Net Positive Economy: Regenerative Business Models, Inclusive Growth, and Sustainable Economic Transformation

Copyright

Net Positive Economy: Regenerative Business Models, Inclusive Growth, and Sustainable Economic Transformation

© 2025 Robert C. Brears

ISBN (eBook): 978-1-991369-61-1

ISBN (Paperback): 978-1-991369-62-8

Published by Global Climate Solutions

First Edition, 2025

Cover design and interior layout by Global Climate Solutions

Table of Contents

Introduction

The world is at a crossroads. Climate change, biodiversity loss, and social inequality are no longer distant threats—they are present-day realities shaping our economies, communities, and future prospects. In response, businesses, governments, and civil society are increasingly seeking solutions that go beyond sustainability as traditionally defined. Doing "less harm" is no longer enough. What's needed now is a systemic shift toward doing more good.

This is the foundation of the Net Positive Economy—an economic model in which organizations and systems give back more to the environment and society than they take. Unlike approaches that focus solely on reducing negative impacts, the net positive concept emphasizes active regeneration of natural capital, restoration of ecosystems, advancement of equity, and long-term resilience. It challenges all sectors to rethink their purpose, redesign their operations, and redefine what success means.

The Net Positive Economy builds on—and evolves from—earlier frameworks such as corporate social responsibility (CSR), environmental, social, and governance (ESG) integration, and sustainability reporting. While these have advanced awareness and disclosure, the net positive approach goes further. It is outcome-oriented, systemic in scope, and grounded in measurable improvements to ecological and human wellbeing.

This book provides a comprehensive yet concise guide to the principles, pathways, and enabling conditions for transitioning to a Net Positive Economy. It is intended for a wide audience: business leaders seeking to embed regeneration into strategy; policymakers working to align growth with environmental limits; investors looking to finance long-term value; civil society actors shaping public discourse; and citizens committed to inclusive and responsible living.

The structure of the book reflects the integrated nature of the net positive framework. It defines core concepts, explores strategic approaches to regenerative resource use and equitable value creation, and outlines the role of finance, innovation, governance, and leadership. The closing chapters examine cultural and behavioral changes that support long-term transformation.

Rather than focusing on specific examples, the book emphasizes generalized frameworks, practical tools, and strategic principles that can be adapted across sectors and geographies. It draws from systems thinking, planetary boundaries, and social foundations to support readers in applying net positive thinking to their own work and context.

The time for incremental change has passed. This book invites the reader to engage with a more ambitious, regenerative, and inclusive model of progress—one that not only meets the needs of the present, but enhances the capacity of future generations to thrive.

Chapter 1: Understanding the Net Positive Economy

This chapter introduces the foundational concepts behind the Net Positive Economy. It outlines how thinking has evolved from corporate social responsibility and traditional sustainability approaches toward a model focused on regeneration and long-term value creation. By exploring the principles that underpin net positive thinking—such as inclusion, resilience, and systems interdependence—the chapter clarifies how this framework differs from related concepts like net zero or carbon neutrality. It also examines the global drivers prompting this shift, including climate risk, resource constraints, and stakeholder expectations. The goal is to provide a clear and structured entry point for understanding what a net positive approach entails and why it is gaining relevance across sectors.

Evolution from CSR and Sustainability to Net Positive Thinking

Corporate responsibility has undergone a series of transitions over the past few decades, reflecting increasing awareness of the environmental and social consequences of business activities. The initial phase was largely characterized by CSR, which focused on philanthropic actions, employee volunteerism, ethical behavior, and compliance with basic environmental and labor standards. These efforts were often reactive, positioned outside core business strategy, and framed as discretionary rather than essential to long-term value creation.

As external pressures mounted—driven by climate change, biodiversity loss, resource constraints, and growing social inequality—the expectations placed on organizations began to shift. Stakeholders, including investors, regulators, consumers, and civil society, demanded more consistent and integrated approaches to managing environmental and social impacts. This shift marked the emergence of sustainability as a strategic imperative. Organizations started embedding ESG considerations into their operations, reporting frameworks, and long-term planning processes.

Sustainability initiatives aimed to reduce harm by improving efficiency, minimizing resource use, and cutting emissions. Frameworks such as the UN Sustainable Development Goals (SDGs), the Global Reporting Initiative (GRI), and the Task Force on Climate-related Financial Disclosures (TCFD) provided structure for setting targets and reporting performance. Despite progress, many sustainability efforts remained focused on harm reduction and risk mitigation rather than systemic restoration or regeneration. The emphasis was often on doing less damage rather than delivering net benefits to the environment and society.

The Net Positive Economy represents the next phase in this progression. Rather than limiting harm, the net positive approach focuses on creating conditions where business activities result in a measurable positive impact. This might include restoring ecosystems, replenishing water resources, sequestering more carbon than emitted, or generating social value that exceeds the footprint of operations. The approach is proactive, not reactive; regenerative, not simply sustainable.

Net positive thinking also reframes the role of business in society. It calls for organizations to move beyond compliance and efficiency toward purpose-driven models that align commercial success with long-term environmental and social wellbeing. This model emphasizes systems thinking, recognizing the interconnected nature of ecological and economic health.

The shift from CSR to sustainability and ultimately to net positive reflects a growing understanding that businesses can—and must— play a central role in shaping resilient, inclusive, and regenerative economies. As global challenges become more complex, the evolution toward net positive thinking provides a strategic path for organizations seeking to remain relevant, trusted, and impactful in the decades ahead.

Core Principles: Regeneration, Inclusion, and Resilience

The Net Positive Economy is built on a foundation of three interrelated principles: regeneration, inclusion, and resilience. These principles shape how organizations design their strategies, assess their impacts, and contribute to long-term value for society and the environment.

Regeneration involves actively restoring and enhancing natural and social systems rather than simply minimizing harm. It reflects a shift from extractive models to practices that renew ecological health and strengthen community wellbeing. In environmental terms, regeneration may include reforestation, soil restoration, or restoring aquatic ecosystems. In social contexts, it may involve reinvesting in underserved areas, supporting indigenous knowledge systems, or improving livelihoods. The goal is not just to slow degradation, but to create conditions where systems are improved as a result of business activities.

Inclusion ensures that the benefits of economic activity are equitably distributed and that all stakeholders—regardless of geography, gender, income, or status—are meaningfully considered in decision-making. This principle calls for businesses to address structural inequalities within their operations, supply chains, and broader economic systems. Examples include fair labor practices, accessible services, diverse leadership, and community engagement. Inclusion also supports social cohesion by addressing gaps in opportunity and voice, helping organizations build trust and legitimacy across stakeholder groups.

Resilience refers to the ability of systems to absorb shocks, adapt to disruptions, and continue functioning effectively under changing conditions. For organizations, resilience includes the flexibility to respond to climate-related events, geopolitical shifts, and market volatility. It also involves contributing to the resilience of the communities and ecosystems in which they operate. Resilience is strengthened through diversity, decentralization, long-term planning, and investment in adaptive capacity. It is not only about surviving disruptions but about learning from them and emerging stronger.

Together, these principles reinforce one another. Regeneration without inclusion may reinforce inequalities, while inclusion without resilience may be vulnerable to disruption. A net positive approach depends on the alignment and integration of all three. Regenerative strategies should be inclusive, and both must be designed to build lasting resilience.

These principles offer a new reference point for evaluating progress. Instead of focusing solely on compliance or incremental improvements, organizations are encouraged to assess whether they are contributing to system-wide restoration, shared prosperity, and long-term stability. As a framework, regeneration, inclusion, and resilience provide a foundation for rethinking business purpose and designing strategies that align with the needs of people and the planet.

The Role of Planetary Boundaries and Social Foundations

A Net Positive Economy is anchored in the understanding that all economic activity operates within the limits of Earth's biophysical systems and the thresholds of social wellbeing. Two essential frameworks—planetary boundaries and social foundations—help define the space within which humanity can thrive without destabilizing natural systems or leaving people behind.

The planetary boundaries framework identifies nine critical Earth system processes that regulate the planet's stability, such as climate change, biodiversity loss, freshwater use, and land-system change. Staying within these boundaries is considered essential to maintaining a safe operating space for humanity. Crossing these thresholds increases the risk of large-scale, potentially irreversible environmental changes that could undermine ecological resilience and human development.

On the other side of the spectrum, social foundations refer to the minimum conditions required for individuals and communities to live with dignity, opportunity, and security. These include access to food, water, energy, healthcare, education, housing, income, and political representation. A failure to meet these foundational needs can result in social fragmentation, inequality, and economic exclusion.

Together, these frameworks form what is often referred to as the "safe and just space for humanity." The concept has gained prominence through models like Doughnut Economics, which visualize the need to operate between an ecological ceiling and a social floor. In this model, economic development is only considered successful if it remains within planetary limits while simultaneously meeting human needs.

A Net Positive Economy integrates this dual perspective by seeking to restore and enhance ecological systems while advancing social equity and inclusion. It moves beyond balancing trade-offs between environment and development, instead striving for outcomes that reinforce both. For example, regenerative agriculture can improve soil health and biodiversity while also supporting livelihoods and food security.

This approach has implications for decision-making across sectors. It requires that organizations assess their strategies not only in terms of financial or operational outcomes but also based on their contribution to global sustainability thresholds and social progress. Metrics, tools, and reporting mechanisms must be aligned with both ecological and human wellbeing.

The integration of planetary boundaries and social foundations transforms how success is defined. It calls for actions that restore critical ecosystems and strengthen communities, rather than merely reducing harm or complying with minimum standards. By grounding economic activity within these scientifically informed and ethically driven parameters, the Net Positive Economy provides a pathway toward long-term resilience and collective prosperity.

Systems Thinking and Interconnectedness of Ecological and Economic Systems

The Net Positive Economy is underpinned by systems thinking—a perspective that recognizes the complex, dynamic relationships between ecological, social, and economic systems. Rather than viewing environmental or social issues in isolation, systems thinking emphasizes the interactions, feedback loops, and dependencies that link various components of the global economy and natural world.

Traditional business models often take a linear approach: resources are extracted, products are manufactured and consumed, and waste is generated. This model tends to externalize environmental and social costs, treating them as unrelated to the core functioning of the economy. Systems thinking challenges this view by highlighting that economic activity is embedded within and dependent upon healthy ecological and social systems.

For example, deforestation may drive short-term economic gain through timber or agricultural production. However, from a systems perspective, it can simultaneously reduce carbon sequestration, disrupt water cycles, threaten biodiversity, and undermine the livelihoods of local communities. These effects may feed back into the economy through increased climate risks, food insecurity, and social instability.

By adopting systems thinking, organizations can better anticipate unintended consequences, identify synergies, and design interventions that deliver benefits across multiple domains. This might include projects that enhance ecosystem services while supporting local employment or infrastructure investments that increase climate resilience and social inclusion.

Systems thinking also encourages a shift from short-term optimization to long-term value creation. It involves understanding the root causes of problems, rather than only addressing symptoms. In the context of the Net Positive Economy, this means aligning business models and policies with the long-term health of the systems they depend on—such as freshwater availability, climate regulation, and community wellbeing.

Additionally, systems thinking supports adaptive management. Complex systems are rarely predictable, and conditions can change rapidly. Organizations that recognize this can build in flexibility, monitor feedback, and adjust their strategies as circumstances evolve. This adaptability enhances resilience and fosters continuous learning.

Embedding systems thinking in the Net Positive Economy helps bridge gaps between sustainability objectives and business decision-making. It fosters cross-sector collaboration, integrated planning, and holistic problem-solving. Rather than compartmentalizing issues into environmental, social, or economic silos, it promotes solutions that reflect the real-world complexity of sustainable development.

Ultimately, systems thinking enables organizations to move beyond fragmented responses and instead contribute to system-level transformation. It is an essential mindset for those aiming to create outcomes that are not only sustainable but also regenerative and inclusive.

Distinction Between Net Zero, Carbon Neutrality, and Net Positive

As businesses and governments accelerate their climate and sustainability commitments, the terms net zero, carbon neutrality, and net positive are often used to describe different levels of ambition. While related, these concepts reflect distinct approaches to managing environmental impacts and should not be used interchangeably.

Carbon neutrality refers to balancing the amount of carbon dioxide emitted with an equivalent amount removed or offset. This typically involves calculating total emissions and purchasing carbon credits to neutralize them. While this can be a useful starting point, the approach does not necessarily require reductions in actual emissions and may rely heavily on offsets, which can vary in credibility and impact.

Net zero, by contrast, requires organizations to reduce greenhouse gas emissions across all scopes—direct, energy-related, and supply chain—by as much as possible, with only the residual emissions being neutralized through verified removal mechanisms. This approach is more rigorous and generally aligned with scientific pathways for limiting global warming to 1.5°C above pre-industrial levels. Net zero is often time-bound, with targets set for 2030 or 2050, and emphasizes decarbonization before offsetting.

Net positive takes the concept further. Instead of aiming for balance, it commits to leaving the environment and society better off as a result of business operations. This could mean restoring more ecosystems than are disrupted, removing more carbon than is emitted, or contributing more to community wellbeing than is consumed. Net positive strategies are proactive, focused on regeneration, and typically extend beyond carbon to include water, biodiversity, social equity, and economic inclusion.

Another key distinction lies in scope and framing. Carbon neutrality and net zero are often treated as compliance or risk mitigation measures, whereas net positive is oriented toward opportunity and contribution. It reframes environmental and social performance as value-generating rather than cost-avoiding. This has implications for business strategy, stakeholder engagement, and brand positioning.

Importantly, a company may achieve net zero emissions while still having a negative impact on ecosystems or communities. Conversely, net positive thinking integrates multiple dimensions of impact into a broader view of sustainability. It encourages systems thinking and recognizes that ecological and human wellbeing are interconnected and mutually reinforcing.

In practice, achieving net positive outcomes requires embedding environmental and social goals into core operations, governance, and innovation processes. It moves beyond reduction and compensation, positioning organizations as contributors to collective progress. As such, the net positive concept represents a more holistic and transformative vision for sustainable development.

Drivers: Climate Risk, Stakeholder Expectations, and Value Creation

Several interrelated drivers are pushing organizations to adopt more ambitious environmental and social strategies aligned with the Net Positive Economy. These include the increasing materiality of climate-related risks, rising stakeholder expectations, and a shift in how long-term value is defined and measured.

Climate risk is now recognized as a core business issue. Physical risks—such as extreme weather, water scarcity, and sea-level rise—are disrupting supply chains, damaging assets, and affecting market access. At the same time, transition risks—such as policy shifts, technological changes, and evolving consumer preferences—are transforming entire industries. Organizations that fail to anticipate and adapt to these changes face financial, legal, and reputational consequences. As a result, climate risk disclosure and scenario planning are becoming standard components of corporate governance and investment analysis.

Stakeholder expectations have also expanded significantly. Investors increasingly seek assurance that companies are managing ESG risks and aligning with sustainability frameworks. Regulators are introducing stricter requirements on emissions reporting, human rights due diligence, and supply chain transparency. Consumers are favoring brands that demonstrate authenticity and social responsibility. Employees—particularly younger generations—are prioritizing purpose and values in their career choices. This multidirectional pressure is pushing companies to go beyond compliance and adopt more proactive, regenerative approaches.

In parallel, the definition of value creation is evolving. Traditional models prioritized short-term financial returns, often at the expense of environmental and social capital. However, there is growing recognition that long-term value depends on the health of the systems that support economic activity. This includes the availability of natural resources, the stability of communities, and the integrity of institutions. Concepts such as integrated reporting, impact investing, and multi-capital accounting are helping organizations measure and communicate value in more comprehensive ways.

For many businesses, these drivers are no longer optional—they are strategic imperatives. Responding to them requires integrating sustainability into core operations, innovation pipelines, and governance structures. It also means shifting from a risk-reduction mindset to one focused on opportunity, differentiation, and leadership.

The Net Positive Economy aligns with this new landscape. It encourages organizations to anticipate change, engage stakeholders meaningfully, and deliver outcomes that go beyond neutrality to contribute actively to societal and ecological wellbeing. In doing so, it positions businesses not just as responders to external pressures, but as agents of systemic transformation.

Chapter 2: Measuring Net Positive Impact

This chapter focuses on how organizations can define, measure, and report net positive outcomes. It reviews key frameworks and indicators across environmental and social domains, highlighting the importance of transparency and consistency in impact accounting. The chapter also introduces multi-capital approaches and tools such as lifecycle assessments and integrated reporting, offering guidance on how to track progress toward regenerative and inclusive goals. Challenges in standardization and verification are discussed, alongside emerging opportunities to strengthen impact measurement systems.

Frameworks for Defining and Quantifying Net Positive Outcomes

Defining and measuring net positive outcomes requires a structured approach that goes beyond conventional ESG reporting. Traditional frameworks often emphasize reducing negative impacts or achieving neutrality, such as reducing emissions or meeting minimum compliance standards. In contrast, a net positive approach seeks to create measurable and lasting improvements in the environment and society that exceed any associated harms.

To achieve this, organizations must begin by establishing clear boundaries around what they intend to measure. This involves defining the scope of impact—whether global, regional, or local—and identifying the relevant domains, such as climate, water, biodiversity, equity, or community wellbeing. These domains must be linked to material issues for the organization and informed by science-based thresholds, policy frameworks, and stakeholder expectations.

The selection of metrics is central to any framework. Net positive outcomes require a shift from input and activity-based metrics to outcome-based indicators. For example, instead of tracking the number of trees planted, a more meaningful metric would assess the ecological function restored or the carbon sequestered over time. Similarly, in the social domain, indicators should capture changes in equity, opportunity, or health outcomes rather than simply counting program beneficiaries.

To ensure credibility and comparability, frameworks should align with emerging global standards and methodologies. These include the Science Based Targets Network (SBTN), Natural Capital Protocol, and the Impact Management Platform. Such initiatives help harmonize terminology, methodologies, and expectations around impact assessment. They also support alignment with the planetary boundaries and social foundations that underpin the concept of a safe and just operating space for humanity.

It is also essential for frameworks to incorporate time-bound targets and baselines. A net positive claim must be evaluated against a defined starting point, such as current environmental conditions or community wellbeing levels. Without this reference, it is difficult to determine whether progress is occurring or whether improvements are attributable to organizational interventions.

Moreover, measurement must reflect causality and attribution. Frameworks should specify how interventions lead to the claimed outcomes and clarify what proportion of the benefit can be attributed to the organization's actions. This is particularly important when partnerships, blended finance, or indirect mechanisms are involved.

Ultimately, frameworks for measuring net positive outcomes must be transparent, science-informed, and adaptive. They should support both internal decision-making and external accountability, helping organizations assess progress, identify gaps, and strengthen impact over time. A well-designed framework is not just a reporting tool; it is a strategic asset that supports continuous improvement and long-term resilience.

Key Performance Indicators Across Environmental and Social Domains

Developing and applying key performance indicators (KPIs) is essential for tracking progress toward net positive outcomes. These indicators serve as the bridge between strategy and implementation, allowing organizations to quantify their contributions and assess whether they are delivering a positive balance of impact across environmental and social domains.

In the environmental domain, KPIs may focus on areas such as carbon, water, biodiversity, and material use. Common indicators include net carbon sequestered, renewable energy generated in excess of operational needs, water replenished beyond consumption, and hectares of habitat restored or protected. These indicators move beyond traditional efficiency metrics by emphasizing regeneration, restoration, and system-wide improvement. For example, a net positive carbon KPI would reflect not only reductions in emissions but also the amount of carbon removed from the atmosphere through verified nature-based or technological solutions.

Social KPIs are equally important and must capture dimensions such as equity, health, education, livelihoods, and inclusion. Examples include increases in living wages across the supply chain, improvements in community health outcomes attributable to organizational programs, or reductions in gender and racial disparities in leadership roles. The goal is to demonstrate positive change in people's lives, not just the number of programs implemented or individuals reached.

Effective KPIs must be measurable, comparable, and aligned with time-bound targets. This requires establishing clear baselines against which progress can be assessed. Baselines might reflect current ecological conditions, historical trends, or globally accepted thresholds such as the SDGs. Targets should be ambitious yet realistic, grounded in science, and reviewed periodically to reflect evolving circumstances and stakeholder expectations.

Another critical aspect is disaggregation. Averages can mask inequalities or localized impacts. Breaking down indicators by region, demographic group, or supply chain tier can provide a more accurate picture of whether net positive goals are being achieved equitably. This is particularly important in the social domain, where generalized results may overlook the needs of marginalized communities.

Organizations should also consider outcome versus output indicators. While outputs reflect activities—such as the number of solar panels installed or workshops delivered—outcomes reflect the actual change achieved, such as emissions avoided or skills gained. Net positive thinking prioritizes outcomes because they represent the real-world impact of interventions.

Finally, credibility and transparency are essential. KPIs should be based on robust methodologies, data quality controls, and, where appropriate, third-party verification. Stakeholders are more likely to trust organizations that are open about their assumptions, data sources, and limitations.

By selecting and managing well-designed KPIs, organizations can move beyond intention to demonstrable impact, ensuring their strategies are delivering net positive results that are both meaningful and measurable.

Multi-Capital Approaches: Natural, Social, Human, and Financial

The Net Positive Economy requires organizations to assess performance through a broader lens than traditional financial accounting allows. The multi-capital approach recognizes that long-term value creation depends on the responsible management of multiple forms of capital—not just financial, but also natural, social, human, and manufactured. Understanding how these capitals interact and influence one another enables organizations to design strategies that deliver systemic, net positive outcomes.

Natural capital refers to the stocks of environmental assets—such as soil, air, water, and biodiversity—that provide essential ecosystem services. These services underpin all economic activity, from food production to climate regulation. A net positive strategy for natural capital involves not only reducing harm but actively enhancing the capacity of ecosystems to function and regenerate over time.

Social capital encompasses the relationships, institutions, norms, and trust that facilitate cooperation within and between communities. Businesses rely on social capital to maintain their social license to operate, engage stakeholders, and support resilient supply chains. Positive contributions to social capital might include strengthening local governance structures, supporting inclusive community development, or building partnerships based on transparency and mutual benefit.

Human capital relates to the health, knowledge, skills, and wellbeing of individuals. It is central to organizational productivity, innovation, and adaptability. A net positive contribution to human capital could involve investing in employee development, promoting mental and physical health, or supporting education and capacity-building in surrounding communities.

Manufactured capital, such as infrastructure, tools, and technology, also plays a role, particularly when aligned with regenerative and inclusive design. While manufactured capital itself is not net positive or negative, how it is used can determine its impact on other capitals. For instance, infrastructure that supports renewable energy, equitable access, and ecological restoration enhances overall value creation.

Financial capital remains important, serving as a means to invest in, allocate, and scale interventions across the other capitals. However, in a net positive framework, financial returns are no longer pursued in isolation. Instead, financial capital is deployed with the intent of producing outcomes that strengthen natural systems, support communities, and build long-term resilience.

Integrating these capitals into decision-making requires tools and frameworks that support holistic accounting. The Integrated Reporting () framework and Natural Capital Protocol offer guidance for assessing and disclosing impacts across multiple capitals. These approaches encourage organizations to consider trade-offs, synergies, and dependencies that would otherwise go unnoticed in single-capital models.

By recognizing and managing value across multiple capitals, organizations can better align their operations with net positive goals. This approach promotes a more complete understanding of impact and fosters strategies that contribute to the health of the systems on which economies and societies depend.

Role of Lifecycle Assessments and Planetary Health Metrics

Accurately measuring net positive outcomes requires tools that assess impacts across the full life cycle of products, services, and operations. Lifecycle Assessment (LCA) is a methodology that provides a comprehensive view of environmental impacts from raw material extraction through production, use, and end-of-life disposal or recycling. In the context of a Net Positive Economy, LCA helps organizations identify not only where harm can be reduced but where value can be added across the supply chain and beyond.

Traditional LCA focuses on environmental metrics such as greenhouse gas emissions, water use, energy consumption, and waste generation. While this is essential for identifying efficiency gains and hotspots, a net positive approach expands the application of LCA to assess regenerative and restorative opportunities. For example, a regenerative farming initiative might demonstrate how soil health improvements sequester carbon over time and enhance water retention, contributing positively to local and global systems.

Complementing lifecycle tools are planetary health metrics, which contextualize organizational impacts within global ecological thresholds. These metrics help determine whether a company's activities contribute to—or detract from—the safe operating space for humanity, as defined by the planetary boundaries framework. Planetary health metrics go beyond relative performance to evaluate whether absolute impacts remain within science-based limits for climate, biodiversity, water, land, and other critical Earth systems.

The integration of planetary health metrics into sustainability strategies enables organizations to align with science-based targets and understand the cumulative impact of their actions. It also supports transparency, comparability, and long-term accountability. For instance, tracking water usage alone is insufficient; understanding whether usage exceeds renewable supply in a specific watershed—thus breaching a planetary boundary—is crucial to assessing sustainability.

Together, LCA and planetary health metrics form a powerful toolkit. LCA provides process-level insights, while planetary metrics offer system-level orientation. Used in tandem, they allow for deeper understanding of where interventions can generate net positive outcomes without shifting burdens elsewhere.

Applying these tools also encourages a mindset shift—from isolated improvements to system-wide thinking. For example, selecting recycled materials may reduce a product's carbon footprint, but if those materials are sourced from a water-stressed region or displace community access, the overall impact may not be positive. Lifecycle and planetary assessments help organizations evaluate these trade-offs and prioritize actions that deliver meaningful and measurable progress.

Incorporating these tools into planning, innovation, and reporting processes enhances the credibility of net positive claims. It demonstrates a commitment to evidence-based decision-making and ensures that environmental improvements are not just symbolic but aligned with the ecological limits of the planet.

Integrated Reporting and Transparent Impact Accounting

Transparency is fundamental to the credibility and effectiveness of net positive strategies. Stakeholders—including investors, regulators, customers, and employees—expect organizations to provide clear, consistent, and comprehensive information about how their activities contribute to environmental and social outcomes. Integrated reporting and impact accounting are tools that support this expectation by aligning financial, environmental, and social performance in a unified narrative.

Integrated reporting refers to the process of combining financial and non-financial data to present a holistic view of an organization's value creation over time. Unlike traditional sustainability reports, which may be published separately from financial statements, integrated reports are intended to show how sustainability is embedded in strategy, governance, and business performance. The Framework developed by the International Integrated Reporting Council provides a widely used structure for disclosing how organizations create, preserve, or erode value across six capitals: financial, manufactured, intellectual, human, social, and natural.

For net positive leaders, integrated reporting is not merely a communication tool—it is an accountability mechanism. It allows organizations to explain their strategic intent, disclose their impact pathways, and demonstrate how they measure progress toward net positive goals. This includes outlining methodologies, baselines, assumptions, and attribution factors. Integrated reporting also encourages forward-looking disclosures, such as scenario analysis, risk assessments, and future targets.

Impact accounting complements integrated reporting by quantifying and valuing environmental and social outcomes. It seeks to assign monetary or non-monetary values to externalities—positive and negative—that arise from business activities. This includes emissions, ecosystem services, labor conditions, and community health impacts. By internalizing these externalities, organizations can make more informed decisions and allocate resources toward high-impact initiatives.

Emerging methodologies, such as the Value Balancing Alliance and Social & Human Capital Protocol, are advancing standards for impact valuation. These frameworks aim to create consistency in how impacts are measured and reported, facilitating comparison across companies and sectors.

Transparency in reporting also supports stakeholder trust. Net positive claims require careful documentation to avoid accusations of "greenwashing" or exaggerated benefits. Third-party assurance, independent reviews, and adherence to recognized reporting standards enhance the legitimacy of disclosed information. Additionally, digital platforms and open data tools can make impact data more accessible and interactive.

Ultimately, integrated reporting and transparent impact accounting signal an organization's commitment to accountability and continuous improvement. They demonstrate that environmental and social impacts are not peripheral considerations, but central to how value is understood, managed, and communicated in a Net Positive Economy.

Challenges and Opportunities in Standardizing Measurement

As the Net Positive Economy gains traction, the demand for reliable, comparable, and transparent measurement is increasing. However, efforts to define and standardize how net positive outcomes are assessed face several challenges. At the same time, these difficulties present opportunities for innovation, collaboration, and leadership.

One major challenge is the lack of common definitions and methodologies. While many organizations have committed to becoming net positive, there is no universally accepted framework that outlines what this means in practice. As a result, different companies may use the same terminology to describe significantly different approaches, metrics, or scopes. This inconsistency can lead to confusion among stakeholders and weaken confidence in reported outcomes.

Attribution and causality also remain difficult to establish. Demonstrating that a specific intervention caused a net positive impact, particularly when multiple actors are involved, requires robust data, baseline analysis, and credible methodologies. The complexity of social and environmental systems adds further uncertainty, especially in cases where impacts are indirect, long-term, or context-specific.

Another issue is the availability and quality of data. Many organizations lack comprehensive systems for collecting data across supply chains, particularly in relation to biodiversity, water impacts, or community wellbeing. Even when data is available, it may be fragmented, inconsistent, or unverifiable. This limits the ability to assess progress, evaluate trade-offs, or report transparently.

Despite these challenges, there are clear opportunities to improve measurement and standardization. Global efforts are underway to align sustainability metrics across sectors. Initiatives such as the Science Based Targets Network, the Taskforce on Nature-related Financial Disclosures (TNFD), and the Impact Management Platform are developing tools, principles, and taxonomies that support more consistent and comparable measurement. These emerging frameworks can guide organizations in selecting appropriate indicators and methodologies, while promoting convergence over time.

Technological advances also offer new possibilities. Satellite imaging, remote sensing, blockchain, and artificial intelligence can help monitor environmental and social outcomes with greater accuracy and efficiency. These tools can improve traceability, reduce costs, and make data more accessible in real time. When combined with digital reporting platforms, they support interactive, dynamic disclosure formats that go beyond static annual reports.

Standardization will also benefit from cross-sector collaboration. Governments, investors, civil society, and businesses all have roles to play in shaping shared expectations and aligning incentives. Engaging with standard-setting bodies and participating in pilot programs can position organizations at the forefront of measurement innovation.

In the long term, resolving measurement challenges will not only increase credibility but also enable more effective strategy development and resource allocation. Standardized, science-based metrics are essential to scaling the Net Positive Economy and ensuring that regenerative and inclusive claims are grounded in verifiable outcomes.

Chapter 3: Regenerative Resource Use

This chapter explores the shift from extractive to regenerative models of resource use. It examines how circular economy principles, renewable resource integration, and systems design can help restore ecosystems while supporting economic activity. The chapter outlines practical strategies for replenishing natural systems—such as water, land, and biodiversity—and discusses policy and market instruments that encourage regenerative practices. It provides a foundation for understanding how resource use can become a source of positive environmental value.

Transition from Extractive to Regenerative Resource Models

Historically, economic growth has been underpinned by extractive models of resource use. These models are based on the linear logic of take–make–dispose, where natural resources are extracted, transformed into products, and ultimately discarded as waste. While this approach has driven industrialization and development, it has also contributed to widespread environmental degradation, biodiversity loss, and climate change. In response, the Net Positive Economy calls for a shift from extractive to regenerative resource models—systems that restore, renew, and enhance the natural capital on which all economies depend.

Regenerative resource models seek to move beyond minimizing harm toward actively creating positive environmental outcomes. This includes practices that improve ecosystem function, enhance biodiversity, rebuild soil fertility, and replenish water cycles. Rather than viewing nature as a passive input, regenerative approaches recognize ecological systems as dynamic partners in sustainable development.

The transition begins with rethinking how materials and energy are sourced. This involves prioritizing renewable resources, reducing dependency on finite materials, and considering the full lifecycle impact of extraction. For example, sourcing wood from certified regenerative forestry programs ensures that forest ecosystems are maintained or improved over time. In agriculture, shifting from chemical-intensive monocultures to regenerative farming systems can enhance soil carbon storage, water retention, and resilience to climate shocks.

Design plays a critical role in this transition. Products and infrastructure must be designed not only for durability and reuse but for environmental regeneration. This includes selecting materials that support circularity, using modular construction to reduce waste, and integrating nature into built environments to provide ecosystem services. Such design choices create systems that restore more than they deplete.

Business models must also adapt. Regenerative resource use requires cross-sector collaboration, long-term thinking, and revised performance metrics. It challenges traditional cost-benefit analyses that prioritize short-term returns over long-term environmental health. Organizations need to develop new capabilities, such as ecosystem restoration planning, ecological monitoring, and stakeholder engagement with local communities and indigenous groups.

Importantly, the transition to regenerative resource models must account for social dimensions. It must be inclusive, respecting the rights and knowledge of those who depend on natural resources for their livelihoods. Regeneration cannot come at the expense of equity or access. Fair benefit-sharing, participatory governance, and capacity-building are all necessary to ensure that regenerative systems are both effective and just.

This shift is not only a sustainability imperative—it is an opportunity for innovation. Regenerative resource models can enhance resilience, reduce long-term costs, and unlock new value streams. As such, they represent a cornerstone of the Net Positive Economy and a pathway toward more balanced, durable, and inclusive prosperity.

Principles of Circular Economy Aligned with Net Positive Goals

The circular economy provides a foundational framework for transitioning from extractive practices to systems that regenerate and restore. While traditional circular economy models focus on reducing waste and improving resource efficiency, a Net Positive Economy builds on these principles by emphasizing outcomes that generate environmental and social value beyond organizational boundaries.

At its core, the circular economy seeks to decouple economic growth from resource consumption. This is achieved by designing out waste and pollution, keeping products and materials in use for as long as possible, and regenerating natural systems. These principles are inherently aligned with net positive thinking, but the key distinction lies in the ambition: where circularity focuses on closing loops, net positive strategies aim to create new loops that deliver net gains to ecosystems and communities.

Design for durability, repair, and reuse is a cornerstone of the circular economy. Extending product life reduces the demand for raw materials and lowers environmental impact across supply chains. In a net positive context, this principle is expanded to ensure that products contribute to regeneration—such as through biodegradable materials that enhance soil health or buildings that support urban biodiversity.

Material recirculation involves recovering and reprocessing materials to retain their value. Recycling is one part of this, but net positive approaches prioritize higher-value strategies such as remanufacturing, refurbishing, and industrial symbiosis—where the by-products of one process become inputs for another. These strategies reduce pressure on natural resources and help close the loop in ways that benefit the environment.

Regeneration of natural systems is the most direct overlap between circular and net positive principles. Circular economy strategies that enhance soil quality, support pollinators, or restore watersheds contribute not only to resilience but also to positive ecological outcomes. These approaches reflect a shift from minimizing footprints to creating handprints—actions that leave a net benefit.

System-wide collaboration is also central to circular and net positive success. Circularity often requires cooperation across value chains, industries, and sectors. Net positive strategies extend this further by involving communities, governments, and non-profits to ensure that social equity and ecological health are embedded in circular designs and outcomes.

While circular economy frameworks often emphasize efficiency and risk reduction, aligning them with net positive goals calls for a broader and more transformative mindset. Organizations must ask not only how to reduce waste or reuse materials, but how to regenerate ecosystems, empower communities, and strengthen resilience through the same processes.

By integrating the principles of circular economy with the intent and outcomes of the Net Positive Economy, organizations can create models of production and consumption that are truly restorative, inclusive, and future-ready.

Strategies for Replenishing Water, Restoring Land, and Enhancing Biodiversity

A core element of regenerative resource use is the commitment to restore critical natural systems. In the context of the Net Positive Economy, this involves moving beyond conservation and mitigation to actively replenish water, restore land, and enhance biodiversity. These efforts contribute directly to ecological resilience and are essential for reversing the degradation caused by extractive development models.

Water replenishment strategies aim to ensure that the quantity and quality of water returned to nature is equal to or greater than what is withdrawn. These strategies include watershed rehabilitation, groundwater recharge, rainwater harvesting, and nature-based solutions such as constructed wetlands. In agricultural or industrial contexts, water reuse, efficiency upgrades, and closed-loop systems reduce demand and allow surplus water to be directed toward ecosystem restoration. For organizations operating in water-stressed areas, replenishment initiatives are particularly impactful and are increasingly expected by regulators and stakeholders.

Land restoration targets degraded landscapes that have lost ecological function due to deforestation, mining, urbanization, or unsustainable farming. Regenerative approaches may involve reforestation, agroforestry, native grassland replanting, erosion control, and soil regeneration. These practices improve carbon sequestration, reduce surface runoff, and restore nutrient cycles. In agricultural settings, regenerative farming techniques—such as cover cropping, composting, and rotational grazing—rebuild topsoil, improve productivity, and reduce dependence on chemical inputs.

Biodiversity enhancement focuses on increasing the variety and abundance of life in ecosystems impacted by human activity. Biodiversity underpins ecosystem services such as pollination, water purification, and climate regulation. Strategies for enhancement include establishing ecological corridors, reintroducing native species, reducing pesticide use, and protecting critical habitats. Urban green infrastructure, such as green roofs and living walls, can support biodiversity in cities while contributing to air quality and cooling.

These three goals—water, land, and biodiversity—are interdependent. For example, restoring wetlands can simultaneously recharge aquifers, provide habitat, and filter pollutants. Likewise, reforesting degraded land can stabilize soil, store carbon, and protect watersheds. Effective strategies are therefore integrated and landscape-based, taking into account local ecological conditions and the broader system context.

To ensure long-term impact, regenerative strategies must be rooted in science and guided by participatory planning. Engaging local communities, indigenous peoples, and other stakeholders can improve outcomes, build local stewardship, and ensure that social and cultural values are respected. Monitoring and adaptive management are also critical to track progress and respond to changing conditions.

Replenishing water, restoring land, and enhancing biodiversity are not only environmental imperatives but also business-relevant strategies. They help reduce operational risks, improve reputation, and open access to sustainability-linked finance. More importantly, they align organizations with the long-term health of the natural systems that underpin economic activity and human wellbeing.

Integrating Renewable Resources in Energy, Materials, and Agriculture

A Net Positive Economy depends on accelerating the shift from finite, polluting resources to renewable ones that can be sustained over the long term. This transition applies across sectors, including energy production, material use, and agricultural systems. The integration of renewable resources supports environmental regeneration, reduces dependence on fossil fuels and resource-intensive inputs, and enhances resilience to global shocks.

In the energy sector, renewable energy—such as solar, wind, hydro, and geothermal—forms the foundation of low-carbon systems. Beyond emissions reduction, net positive strategies aim to produce more renewable energy than consumed or to enable others to transition through investments in offsite generation. Organizations can support this goal through power purchase agreements, on-site generation, grid decentralization, and energy-sharing platforms. Integrating energy storage, smart grids, and demand-side management further increases system efficiency and reliability.

For materials, renewable inputs such as bio-based polymers, responsibly sourced wood, and agricultural by-products offer alternatives to non-renewable and high-impact materials. However, a net positive approach demands that the use of renewables does not result in land degradation, water depletion, or biodiversity loss. Sustainable sourcing standards and full life-cycle assessments are essential to ensure renewable materials are harvested at rates and in ways that allow ecosystems to recover. Prioritizing second-generation materials—such as those derived from agricultural waste—can help reduce land-use conflicts between food, fuel, and fiber production.

In agriculture, the integration of renewable inputs is central to regenerative systems. This includes using organic fertilizers, compost, biological pest control, and renewable energy for irrigation and processing. Renewable practices also encompass ecological crop rotations, diversified planting systems, and reduced reliance on synthetic inputs. These strategies restore soil health, reduce emissions, and improve the adaptive capacity of farming systems. Transitioning to renewable-based agriculture enhances food security while reducing the sector's environmental footprint.

Cross-sector approaches are often the most effective. For example, agricultural residues can be used as feedstock for renewable energy, creating synergies between sectors. Similarly, regenerative forestry can supply both renewable materials and energy while supporting biodiversity and water regulation.

Policy incentives and technological innovation play a vital role in scaling renewable resource use. Feed-in tariffs, green public procurement, and carbon pricing can shift market dynamics, while innovation in bioengineering, material science, and decentralized energy systems opens new possibilities. Organizations can lead by setting ambitious targets for renewable content, supporting supplier transitions, and disclosing progress transparently.

Ultimately, integrating renewable resources is not only about substitution—it is about rethinking systems to operate within ecological limits while restoring the natural capital they depend on. In doing so, businesses contribute to climate mitigation, ecosystem regeneration, and the broader goals of a Net Positive Economy.

Designing Out Waste and Pollution Through Systems Innovation

Eliminating waste and pollution is a foundational principle of regenerative resource use. In the Net Positive Economy, this objective goes beyond conventional waste management to encompass system-level innovation—reimagining how products, services, and entire value chains are designed to prevent environmental degradation before it occurs.

Traditional linear models treat waste and pollution as inevitable by-products of production and consumption. In contrast, net positive thinking calls for designing systems where waste is either eliminated altogether or transformed into a resource. This proactive approach requires addressing problems at the source rather than managing their consequences downstream.

Product design is a critical intervention point. By selecting materials that are non-toxic, biodegradable, or infinitely recyclable, designers can ensure that products do not generate harmful emissions or persistent waste. Modular design and component standardization allow for easier repair, refurbishment, and disassembly. This extends product life, reduces material intensity, and facilitates closed-loop systems. For example, electronic devices designed for modular upgrades can avoid early obsolescence and reduce e-waste volumes.

Process innovation is equally important. Lean manufacturing techniques, precision agriculture, and clean production methods can minimize resource inputs and eliminate unnecessary outputs. Advances in digital technologies—such as sensors, real-time monitoring, and AI-driven analytics—enable organizations to identify inefficiencies and make rapid adjustments to reduce waste across operations.

Pollution prevention strategies focus on avoiding contamination of air, water, and soil. This includes reducing chemical use, capturing emissions at the source, and adopting circular chemistry approaches that prioritize safe, recoverable substances. In agriculture, shifting away from synthetic fertilizers and pesticides toward organic inputs helps protect ecosystems and prevent nutrient runoff.

Value chain collaboration plays a central role in system-wide waste elimination. Organizations can work with suppliers and partners to design packaging that is reusable or compostable, implement take-back schemes, and develop shared infrastructure for material recovery. Industrial symbiosis models, where waste streams from one company serve as inputs for another, turn what was once discarded into a valuable asset.

Consumer engagement also matters. Designing products and services that promote responsible use, care, and disposal can reduce post-consumer waste. Business models based on leasing, sharing, or product-as-a-service concepts shift incentives toward longevity and reuse.

Importantly, systems innovation requires a shift in mindset—from optimizing isolated processes to rethinking entire systems for circularity and regeneration. It demands cross-disciplinary collaboration, long-term planning, and a willingness to disrupt established practices.

Designing out waste and pollution aligns with net positive objectives by preventing harm while creating opportunities for regeneration. It reduces environmental liabilities, enhances resource efficiency, and builds the foundation for economic systems that are restorative by design.

Policy and Market Incentives for Regenerative Practices

The transition to regenerative resource use is unlikely to scale without the support of effective policy frameworks and well-aligned market incentives. While many businesses are advancing regenerative practices voluntarily, enabling conditions must be created to reward positive outcomes, internalize externalities, and lower the risks and costs associated with innovation.

Public policy plays a vital role in shaping market behavior. Regulatory frameworks that restrict pollution, mandate sustainable land use, or enforce water management standards can set minimum baselines for environmental protection. However, in a Net Positive Economy, policies are also expected to enable and accelerate actions that go beyond compliance. This includes offering incentives for ecosystem restoration, biodiversity conservation, and climate-positive agriculture.

Subsidies and tax incentives are among the most direct tools for encouraging regenerative practices. Governments can provide financial support for renewable energy projects, regenerative farming, afforestation, and circular product design. Tax credits or reduced levies on sustainable products and services lower the cost barrier for early adopters, while levies on pollution, resource extraction, or land degradation can discourage harmful practices.

Payments for ecosystem services (PES) offer another mechanism, where landowners or businesses are compensated for providing environmental benefits such as carbon sequestration, water purification, or habitat preservation. PES schemes, whether publicly or privately funded, can make restoration economically viable and provide recurring income to communities engaged in land stewardship.

Green public procurement allows governments to use their purchasing power to stimulate demand for regenerative goods and services. By prioritizing suppliers that meet environmental and social criteria, public institutions can shift entire markets and support the development of green industries. Standards, certification schemes, and ecolabels can complement procurement policies by ensuring transparency and comparability.

Market-based instruments, such as carbon pricing, biodiversity credits, and tradable water rights, help internalize the environmental costs and benefits of resource use. When designed effectively, these instruments create financial incentives for innovation and allow businesses to capture value from positive environmental performance. However, safeguards must be in place to ensure credibility, prevent unintended consequences, and avoid inequities in access or distribution.

Finance and investment markets are also key enablers. Blended finance structures, sustainability-linked loans, and green bonds can unlock capital for regenerative projects that may be high-risk or long-term in nature. Risk-sharing mechanisms and public-private partnerships can further reduce barriers to entry for smaller actors or those in emerging markets.

For policies and incentives to succeed, they must be predictable, consistent, and based on measurable outcomes. Stakeholder engagement is essential to ensure that incentives are fair, inclusive, and contextually appropriate. Aligning policy with scientific evidence, global goals, and local realities enhances effectiveness and builds trust.

When policy and market signals support regeneration, they shift the landscape from one of voluntary leadership to mainstream adoption. This enables businesses to scale their efforts, investors to allocate capital more efficiently, and societies to benefit from the environmental and social value that regenerative systems can provide.

Chapter 4: Inclusive and Equitable Value Creation

This chapter examines how net positive strategies must prioritize equity alongside regeneration. It addresses the importance of economic inclusion, labor fairness, and stakeholder-centered business models. Topics include community wealth-building, supply chain transparency, and bridging global inequalities in development outcomes. The chapter highlights how aligning social equity with regenerative practices enhances resilience and ensures that benefits are shared broadly across populations and regions.

Economic Inclusion as a Pillar of the Net Positive Model

A Net Positive Economy is not only about ecological restoration—it also requires inclusive economic systems that expand opportunities, reduce structural inequities, and ensure that the benefits of growth are shared across all segments of society. Economic inclusion is therefore a central pillar of the net positive model, recognizing that long-term prosperity and resilience cannot be achieved without addressing social and economic disparities.

Traditional economic models have often prioritized aggregate growth over equitable distribution. As a result, gains in productivity and innovation have frequently been accompanied by rising inequality, precarious employment, and marginalization of certain populations. A net positive approach challenges this paradigm by emphasizing fairness, access, and empowerment alongside environmental outcomes.

In practical terms, economic inclusion involves creating conditions where all individuals—regardless of income level, gender, ethnicity, age, or location—can participate meaningfully in economic life. This includes access to decent work, fair wages, financial services, digital infrastructure, education, and decision-making processes. It also involves actively removing barriers that exclude disadvantaged or underrepresented groups from these opportunities.

Businesses have a significant role to play in advancing inclusion. Inclusive hiring practices, supplier diversity programs, and investment in workforce development can contribute to more equitable labor markets. Organizations can support local enterprises, particularly in underserved areas, by facilitating access to capital, skills, and networks. In doing so, they help build economic ecosystems that are more resilient and self-sustaining.

At the community level, inclusive approaches may involve participatory planning, revenue-sharing mechanisms, or co-designed service delivery models that ensure that benefits align with local needs and values. This is especially important in contexts where infrastructure projects or natural resource use intersect with indigenous lands or low-income neighborhoods.

Financial inclusion is another key dimension. Expanding access to credit, insurance, savings, and mobile banking enables individuals and small businesses to build assets, manage risks, and invest in their futures. Innovations in fintech, microfinance, and social enterprise models have demonstrated how financial tools can be deployed to close economic gaps.

Importantly, inclusion is not only a matter of ethics—it is also a strategic advantage. Diverse organizations tend to be more innovative, adaptable, and aligned with stakeholder expectations. Inclusive growth supports social cohesion, reduces political and market risk, and strengthens institutional legitimacy.

In a Net Positive Economy, inclusion is both an outcome and an enabler. It ensures that the transition to regenerative and low-carbon systems is socially just, that communities have agency in shaping their futures, and that no one is left behind. By embedding inclusion in policies, business strategies, and investment decisions, organizations contribute to a more equitable and sustainable global economy.

Labor Equity, Fair Wages, and Stakeholder Capitalism

A Net Positive Economy depends on more than environmental outcomes—it requires a fundamental commitment to labor equity and fair wages across all levels of economic activity. These components ensure that workers are treated with dignity, rewarded appropriately, and included in shaping the decisions that affect their lives. Embedded within this approach is the broader concept of stakeholder capitalism, which prioritizes the interests of all stakeholders—not just shareholders—as essential to long-term value creation.

Labor equity refers to the fair treatment of workers regardless of gender, race, ethnicity, age, ability, or employment status. It involves ensuring equal access to opportunities, eliminating discrimination, and fostering inclusive workplace cultures. In a net positive context, this means going beyond compliance with legal requirements to proactively address structural inequities and unconscious biases that may exist within recruitment, promotion, and compensation practices.

Fair wages are a cornerstone of labor equity. Too often, economic growth has been accompanied by stagnating real incomes for low- and middle-income workers. A net positive organization commits to paying living wages that meet the basic needs of workers and their families. This extends across direct employees, contractors, and the supply chain. Transparent wage policies, collective bargaining rights, and regular wage assessments are key practices in advancing fair compensation.

Safe and healthy working conditions are also essential. This includes not only physical safety but also mental health and work-life balance. Access to benefits such as paid leave, healthcare, and family support services contributes to the overall wellbeing of workers and enhances organizational performance through improved morale and retention.

Stakeholder capitalism provides the governance framework for integrating labor considerations into business strategy. Unlike shareholder primacy, which focuses on maximizing short-term profits, stakeholder capitalism recognizes employees, suppliers, customers, communities, and the environment as integral to the success of the enterprise. Under this model, boards and executives are accountable for delivering shared value and managing trade-offs in a transparent and participatory manner.

Practically, this may involve stakeholder representation in governance processes, inclusive impact assessments, or employee ownership models. Companies may also disclose social performance indicators alongside financial results to demonstrate alignment with stakeholder interests.

Labor equity and stakeholder capitalism are particularly important in the context of the green transition. As economies shift toward renewable energy, circular systems, and low-carbon infrastructure, workers in legacy sectors may face displacement. Net positive strategies address this by investing in just transition programs that provide retraining, income support, and pathways into new industries.

By advancing labor equity and adopting stakeholder capitalism, organizations not only strengthen their social license to operate but also build more resilient, innovative, and adaptive institutions. In doing so, they help ensure that the benefits of a net positive future are both sustainable and widely shared.

Community Wealth-Building and Inclusive Governance

In a Net Positive Economy, economic development is not measured solely by corporate profitability or GDP growth but by the extent to which prosperity is shared and sustained at the local level. Community wealth-building and inclusive governance are essential mechanisms for achieving this, ensuring that economic activity strengthens local economies, fosters long-term resilience, and empowers people to participate meaningfully in decisions that affect their lives.

Community wealth-building is a place-based approach to economic development that focuses on retaining and circulating wealth within local economies. It emphasizes ownership models that keep value anchored in communities, such as cooperatives, employee-owned firms, social enterprises, and locally rooted anchor institutions like hospitals and universities. By supporting community-controlled assets, this approach reduces economic leakage, builds financial resilience, and creates inclusive opportunities for work and entrepreneurship.

Public procurement strategies can play a powerful role in community wealth-building. Governments and large organizations can redirect spending to local suppliers, minority-owned businesses, or mission-aligned enterprises, thereby stimulating local job creation and enterprise development. Likewise, community investment funds and participatory budgeting initiatives can channel financial resources toward priorities identified by residents themselves.

Inclusive governance ensures that the voices of community members—particularly those historically excluded—are represented in decision-making processes. This includes planning, resource allocation, and policy development. Participatory processes, such as citizen assemblies, stakeholder councils, and community-led planning forums, promote transparency and accountability while fostering trust between institutions and the public.

Effective inclusive governance recognizes and values local knowledge. Community members often possess deep understanding of their ecological, social, and cultural contexts, which can improve the relevance and sustainability of development interventions. For example, involving indigenous communities in land-use planning can enhance conservation outcomes while respecting cultural heritage and land rights.

Incorporating inclusive governance into business practices requires shifting from a transactional to a relational approach with communities. Rather than viewing stakeholders solely as beneficiaries or consumers, businesses engage communities as co-creators of value. This may involve long-term partnerships, joint ventures, or shared governance models, especially where projects have significant environmental or social footprints.

Importantly, community wealth-building and inclusive governance are not only relevant in rural or under-resourced settings. In urban areas, similar principles apply to housing cooperatives, community land trusts, and neighborhood-based economic development strategies that ensure gentrification and growth do not displace existing residents.

These approaches contribute to a Net Positive Economy by embedding equity, resilience, and local empowerment at the heart of economic systems. When communities are enabled to retain wealth and shape their own futures, they are better positioned to adapt to environmental challenges, attract investment, and foster inclusive, long-term prosperity.

Supply Chain Transparency and Social Justice in Sourcing

Supply chains are central to the global economy, but they often obscure the environmental and social conditions under which goods and services are produced. In a Net Positive Economy, supply chain transparency and social justice in sourcing are critical for ensuring that regenerative and inclusive outcomes extend beyond an organization's direct operations and into the broader network of suppliers and contractors.

Supply chain transparency involves mapping, monitoring, and disclosing information about suppliers, sourcing locations, labor practices, environmental performance, and risks throughout the value chain. Visibility into upstream and downstream activities enables organizations to identify areas of concern, take corrective action, and communicate openly with stakeholders about their impact. Tools such as traceability platforms, digital ledgers, and satellite monitoring are increasingly used to enhance transparency, especially in complex global supply chains.

Transparency is a prerequisite for accountability. Without access to reliable data, it is difficult to assess whether sourcing practices align with net positive principles or contribute to deforestation, forced labor, land grabs, or pollution. Transparency also supports ethical consumer behavior and investor decision-making by providing credible information on how products are made and sourced.

Social justice in sourcing means actively addressing inequalities, exploitation, and exclusion in supply chains. This includes ensuring that workers are paid fairly, operate in safe conditions, and have the right to organize. It also involves respecting indigenous land rights, securing the free, prior, and informed consent (FPIC) of affected communities, and ensuring that smallholder farmers, women, and minority-owned businesses have equitable access to market opportunities.

Responsible sourcing frameworks such as Fair Trade, Rainforest Alliance, and the Ethical Trading Initiative set minimum standards, but net positive sourcing goes further. It seeks to create positive impacts—such as improving livelihoods, enhancing food security, or strengthening community infrastructure—as a result of commercial relationships. This may involve capacity-building programs, long-term contracts, or co-investment in regenerative practices by suppliers.

Effective implementation requires collaboration across the supply chain. Buyers must engage suppliers as partners in continuous improvement, not simply as cost centers. This can include providing technical assistance, supporting certification efforts, and recognizing leadership in social and environmental performance. Tier 1 suppliers should also be encouraged to cascade similar expectations to their own partners.

Governments and industry associations are increasingly mandating greater supply chain due diligence, particularly related to human rights and environmental harm. Anticipating and aligning with these regulations can position businesses as proactive leaders and reduce reputational and legal risk.

By promoting transparency and justice in sourcing, organizations help build more resilient, inclusive, and ethical supply chains. These practices not only reduce harm but can also create shared value and deepen trust with stakeholders. In doing so, they extend the reach of net positive commitments across the full lifecycle of products and services.

Bridging the Global North–South Gap in Economic Outcomes

One of the most persistent features of the global economy is the uneven distribution of wealth, resources, and opportunities between the Global North and Global South. A Net Positive Economy recognizes the importance of bridging this divide to create more balanced, resilient, and inclusive global systems. Addressing historical and structural imbalances is essential not only for equity but for achieving shared progress on sustainability and regeneration goals.

The Global North, comprising high-income, industrialized countries, has historically benefited from economic systems that extract value—whether natural resources, labor, or intellectual property—from the Global South, which includes many low- and middle-income nations. These dynamics have often resulted in wealth accumulation in the North and underdevelopment, environmental degradation, or debt burdens in the South.

Bridging this gap requires more than development aid or charity. It involves shifting toward models of partnership, equity, and mutual benefit. One approach is to ensure that value chains are structured so that greater value is retained at the source. This includes supporting local processing and manufacturing, ensuring fair pricing for commodities, and enabling local ownership of productive assets.

Technology transfer and capacity building are also critical. Many sustainability innovations—whether in renewable energy, digital agriculture, or climate adaptation—are developed in the Global North. Making these technologies accessible, affordable, and adaptable for use in the Global South accelerates global progress while reducing dependency. Capacity building complements this by strengthening local institutions, governance systems, and knowledge networks.

Climate finance is another area of focus. The Global South is often the most vulnerable to climate impacts, despite contributing the least to global emissions. Fair and effective climate finance mechanisms—such as concessional loans, grants, and blended finance—can support investments in resilience, mitigation, and adaptation. Ensuring that these flows are predictable, transparent, and aligned with national priorities is key to enabling country-led sustainable development.

Trade and investment policies must also be examined. Trade agreements and investment frameworks can unintentionally perpetuate extractive practices or limit policy space for countries in the Global South. Reforms that support fair trade, remove harmful subsidies, and promote sustainable production standards can improve development outcomes while advancing net positive goals.

Importantly, these efforts must be guided by the principles of sovereignty, respect, and collaboration. Solutions that are imposed without regard for local contexts or priorities risk reinforcing the very inequalities they seek to address. Instead, inclusive dialogue and co-creation of solutions can help foster trust, legitimacy, and durable partnerships.

By bridging the Global North–South gap, the Net Positive Economy contributes to a more just and sustainable world. It enables more countries and communities to participate in, benefit from, and lead the transition to regenerative economic systems.

Aligning Equity and Regenerative Growth

For a Net Positive Economy to succeed, equity and regenerative growth must be pursued not as parallel goals but as mutually reinforcing objectives. Aligning the two ensures that environmental regeneration does not come at the expense of social justice—and that efforts to promote inclusion are grounded in the ecological limits of the planet. This alignment represents a shift from traditional models of growth toward integrated strategies that recognize the interdependence of people and the environment.

Historically, economic growth has often led to resource depletion, environmental degradation, and increased inequality. In contrast, regenerative growth aims to restore ecological systems while improving social outcomes. This includes building inclusive institutions, advancing participatory governance, and creating livelihoods that are not only sustainable but dignified and empowering.

Equity in regenerative systems means ensuring that all communities—especially those historically marginalized—have access to the benefits of regeneration. This includes equitable access to clean energy, green infrastructure, healthy environments, and economic opportunities in emerging sectors such as renewable energy, ecosystem restoration, and circular manufacturing. It also involves addressing legacy harms, such as environmental injustice in low-income neighborhoods or land dispossession among Indigenous peoples.

Inclusive decision-making is central to this alignment. Regenerative projects, whether urban greening or rural reforestation, must be developed with community input and oversight. Doing so ensures that projects reflect local priorities and values, avoids unintended consequences, and builds local ownership and stewardship.

Economic policies can support this alignment by integrating social equity into environmental incentive structures. For example, carbon pricing revenues can be redistributed to support vulnerable households, while subsidies for regenerative agriculture can prioritize smallholder and women farmers. These approaches help ensure that environmental progress does not exacerbate inequality, but instead contributes to systemic fairness.

At the organizational level, aligning equity and regeneration means adopting frameworks that incorporate both social and environmental performance. This includes integrated impact measurement, inclusive stakeholder engagement, and leadership accountability for equity outcomes. Companies can set dual targets—for example, increasing representation in green jobs while restoring degraded ecosystems—ensuring that social inclusion and ecological restoration advance together.

Education and workforce development are also critical. Preparing people for the regenerative economy requires investment in training, lifelong learning, and career pathways in fields such as sustainable construction, ecosystem services, and clean energy. This helps close opportunity gaps and supports a just transition for workers in high-emissions sectors.

Ultimately, aligning equity with regenerative growth reflects a broader redefinition of prosperity—one that measures success not only in financial terms, but in the health of communities and ecosystems. It recognizes that resilience and sustainability are strongest when grounded in fairness and shared responsibility. In doing so, it charts a course toward a Net Positive Economy that is inclusive by design and regenerative in impact.

Chapter 5: Finance for a Net Positive Future

This chapter discusses the role of financial systems in supporting the Net Positive Economy. It explores tools such as green, blue, and sustainability-linked finance, and compares different approaches including ESG investing, impact investing, and net positive finance. The chapter highlights the importance of aligning risk-adjusted returns with long-term system value and outlines financial mechanisms that can support regeneration. It also examines how transition finance and divestment strategies are shaping capital allocation decisions.

Role of Green, Blue, and Sustainability-Linked Finance

Finance plays a pivotal role in scaling the Net Positive Economy. The allocation of capital determines which projects are developed, which technologies are commercialized, and which business models succeed. As environmental and social risks become more material to financial markets, green, blue, and sustainability-linked finance mechanisms are increasingly being used to direct funding toward outcomes that contribute positively to nature and society.

Green finance refers to financial products and investment flows that support environmental objectives, particularly climate mitigation and adaptation. This includes green bonds, green loans, and green investment funds that finance activities such as renewable energy, energy efficiency, sustainable transport, and ecosystem restoration. These instruments often follow established taxonomies or certification schemes to ensure the environmental integrity of the financed activities.

Blue finance is an emerging field that applies the principles of green finance to ocean and freshwater systems. It supports projects that enhance marine biodiversity, protect coastal ecosystems, improve water quality, or develop sustainable fisheries and aquaculture.

Examples include blue bonds for coral reef restoration, investments in climate-resilient coastal infrastructure, and credit schemes for reducing plastic pollution in waterways. As awareness grows of the economic and ecological importance of aquatic ecosystems, blue finance is gaining recognition as a critical tool for net positive impact.

Sustainability-linked finance ties the terms of a financial product—such as interest rates or covenants—to an organization's performance on predefined environmental or social indicators. Unlike green or blue instruments, which finance specific projects, sustainability-linked instruments can support general corporate purposes while incentivizing improved performance. If the borrower fails to meet the targets (e.g., reducing emissions or improving gender equity), financial penalties may apply; if targets are met or exceeded, favorable terms may be granted.

These financial tools are helping to mainstream sustainability considerations across banking, asset management, and insurance. They provide investors and lenders with a structured way to support companies that are aligned with net positive principles. They also encourage issuers to set ambitious, time-bound targets and disclose their progress transparently.

However, to fulfill their potential, these instruments must be credible, transparent, and aligned with science-based pathways. Independent verification, robust use-of-proceeds tracking, and clear impact reporting are essential to guard against greenwashing and maintain market confidence. Coordination among standard-setters, financial regulators, and rating agencies is also important to ensure consistency and comparability.

As demand grows for investments that generate measurable positive outcomes, green, blue, and sustainability-linked finance will continue to evolve. They offer a vital means of channeling capital toward the regenerative systems that underpin a Net Positive

Economy—and in doing so, they redefine financial performance as both a return on investment and a return to society and the planet.

ESG Investing vs. Impact Investing vs. Net Positive Finance

The financial sector has seen the rapid emergence of a range of investment approaches aimed at integrating environmental and social considerations into decision-making. Among the most prominent are ESG investing, impact investing, and, more recently, approaches aligned with net positive finance. While these categories are often discussed together, they represent different levels of ambition, methodology, and outcome orientation.

ESG investing focuses on integrating environmental, social, and governance risks and opportunities into traditional investment analysis. It is primarily concerned with how sustainability factors affect financial performance. Investors may exclude companies with high ESG risks or overweight those with strong ESG scores. ESG integration can support better risk-adjusted returns by avoiding exposure to environmental liabilities, regulatory penalties, or reputational damage. However, ESG investing does not necessarily seek to generate positive environmental or social impact. In many cases, it is a tool for improving financial resilience rather than advancing regeneration or inclusion.

Impact investing moves beyond risk management to explicitly pursue measurable social and environmental outcomes alongside financial returns. Impact investors typically allocate capital to projects, enterprises, or funds that deliver targeted results—such as improved health outcomes, increased renewable energy access, or education for underserved communities. Impact investing requires intentionality, measurability, and reporting, and is often aligned with the United Nations SDGs. The impact investing market has grown significantly in recent years, with institutional and philanthropic capital increasingly entering the space.

Net positive finance builds on the impact investing mindset but applies it at a more systemic level. Rather than focusing on minimizing harm or achieving discrete impacts, net positive finance aims to fund activities and institutions that create a net gain for people and the planet—leaving ecosystems healthier and societies more equitable than before. This could include financing regenerative agriculture, restoring degraded ecosystems, or investing in companies that produce more clean energy than they consume. The focus is on outcomes that contribute more than they extract, aligned with planetary boundaries and social foundations.

Net positive finance also emphasizes the need for structural change in financial systems. This includes shifting incentives, redefining fiduciary duty to include long-term planetary health, and reforming capital markets to reward regeneration. It calls for new metrics, governance models, and accountability mechanisms that align financial flows with environmental and social thresholds.

While ESG investing is becoming mainstream and impact investing is expanding, net positive finance remains at an early stage. However, it offers a vision for the future of finance—one in which capital is not just managed for returns or screened for risks, but actively directed toward building a regenerative and inclusive economy.

Each approach plays a role in the broader transition. Understanding their distinctions—and how they can evolve—is key to aligning investment strategies with the ambition and urgency of the Net Positive Economy.

Risk-Adjusted Returns and Long-Term Value Alignment

In the context of the Net Positive Economy, investment performance is not only measured by short-term gains but by how well financial decisions align with long-term environmental, social, and economic value. The concept of risk-adjusted returns—a standard in financial analysis—must therefore evolve to incorporate broader definitions of risk and value. This shift supports the alignment of capital with regenerative and inclusive outcomes while still meeting institutional expectations for return on investment.

Traditional risk-adjusted return models focus primarily on financial volatility and downside exposure. These models assess the likelihood of underperformance relative to a benchmark, adjusting for market, credit, and liquidity risk. While useful, such models often overlook systemic risks that could impact long-term asset performance—including climate change, ecosystem collapse, social unrest, and regulatory shifts.

Increasingly, investors are recognizing environmental and social risks as material financial risks. Physical climate risks (e.g., droughts, floods, wildfires), transitional risks (e.g., carbon pricing, technology disruption), and social risks (e.g., labor rights violations, inequality) can significantly impact company performance, asset valuations, and portfolio resilience. Integrating these risks into financial modeling improves the accuracy of risk assessments and supports more informed decision-making.

At the same time, investors are paying greater attention to opportunity alignment—the ability of assets to benefit from the transition to a sustainable economy. This includes exposure to sectors such as renewable energy, nature-based solutions, inclusive housing, or circular manufacturing. Investments aligned with long-term trends are more likely to deliver consistent returns, attract support from stakeholders, and avoid stranded asset risk.

Aligning with long-term value also requires moving beyond conventional metrics. Tools such as scenario analysis, internal carbon pricing, and natural capital accounting enable investors to assess how assets perform under different future conditions. Portfolio alignment tools—such as the Paris Agreement Capital Transition Assessment (PACTA) and science-based investment targets—help investors evaluate the degree to which their portfolios support global climate and biodiversity goals.

Time horizon is a key factor. Short-term market movements may not fully reflect the risks or benefits of net positive strategies. Institutional investors with longer time frames—such as pension funds, sovereign wealth funds, and endowments—are well-positioned to adopt investment approaches that emphasize durability, resilience, and systemic value creation.

Importantly, aligning with long-term value does not require sacrificing returns. Many studies show that companies with strong sustainability performance outperform their peers over time. By avoiding downside risk, accessing new markets, and enhancing stakeholder trust, net positive strategies can support financial outperformance while delivering broader societal and environmental benefits.

In a Net Positive Economy, risk-adjusted returns reflect the full spectrum of impacts—financial, environmental, and social. Aligning capital with this expanded understanding of value is essential to managing risk, capturing opportunity, and building resilient financial systems for the future.

Financial Mechanisms to Support Regeneration

Achieving the goals of a Net Positive Economy requires a financial system capable of funding activities that restore natural systems, enhance community resilience, and promote equitable development. A range of financial mechanisms—from grants and concessional loans to blended finance and market-based instruments—can be deployed to support regenerative outcomes. These tools help channel capital toward projects and sectors that may not yet be competitive under traditional risk-return expectations but offer long-term social and environmental value.

Grants and concessional finance remain important for early-stage regenerative initiatives, particularly in developing economies or in sectors with uncertain commercial viability. These funds can be used to de-risk projects, build capacity, and support innovation in areas such as regenerative agriculture, forest restoration, or climate-resilient infrastructure. Multilateral development banks and philanthropic organizations often play a central role in providing this type of support.

Blended finance combines concessional funding with private investment to improve the bankability of regenerative projects. For example, a concessional loan or first-loss guarantee might attract private lenders to a reforestation project by reducing their exposure to downside risk. This approach is increasingly used in sustainable development and climate finance, with platforms such as the Global Environment Facility (GEF) and Green Climate Fund (GCF) facilitating such arrangements.

Debt-for-nature swaps offer a targeted mechanism for regenerative finance in countries with high debt burdens and valuable ecosystems. Under these arrangements, a portion of a country's external debt is forgiven in exchange for commitments to invest in conservation or ecosystem restoration. These transactions not only alleviate fiscal pressure but also generate lasting environmental and social benefits when well-designed and monitored.

Payment for ecosystem services (PES) creates financial incentives for landholders and communities to manage land in ways that generate public goods—such as clean water, carbon sequestration, or biodiversity protection. PES schemes can be funded by governments, private companies, or environmental markets, and they are particularly effective in encouraging the adoption of regenerative practices in agriculture and forestry.

Sustainability-linked loans and bonds, discussed earlier, can also support regeneration by tying financial terms to outcomes such as increased tree cover, improved water retention, or reduction in pesticide use. When metrics are aligned with regenerative goals and independently verified, these instruments create incentives for borrowers to exceed minimum standards and invest in systemic restoration.

Green investment funds and natural capital funds are growing in size and scope, providing equity and debt finance for projects that deliver ecological and financial returns. These vehicles often focus on scalable interventions, such as habitat banking, regenerative aquaculture, or sustainable forestry, and may be structured to attract institutional investors through clear risk-return profiles.

Scaling these mechanisms requires coordinated efforts among public institutions, private investors, and civil society. Standardized methodologies, robust impact measurement, and supportive regulatory frameworks are essential for building trust and ensuring effectiveness.

Financial mechanisms that support regeneration are not just about mobilizing capital—they are about restructuring financial flows to reward actions that improve ecological and human systems. By embedding regeneration into financial decision-making, these tools help create a foundation for sustainable prosperity and long-term resilience.

Transition Financing and Divestment Strategies

In the journey toward a Net Positive Economy, financial institutions and investors play a critical role in both enabling change and phasing out harmful practices. This dual responsibility involves deploying transition financing to support industries and regions in moving toward sustainability, while also using divestment strategies to reallocate capital away from activities that undermine environmental and social systems.

Transition financing refers to capital specifically allocated to help carbon-intensive sectors and legacy business models reduce their environmental footprint over time. This includes industries such as steel, cement, aviation, shipping, and agriculture—sectors that are essential to the global economy but face significant challenges in decarbonizing or reducing ecological impact. Transition finance supports investments in cleaner technologies, process improvements, energy efficiency, and workforce reskilling, enabling companies to shift their operations in line with science-based targets.

Rather than immediately withdrawing financial support from hard-to-abate sectors, transition financing provides a pathway for companies to make meaningful progress. However, it must be accompanied by clear expectations, accountability, and time-bound performance indicators. Without rigorous standards, there is a risk that transition finance will be used to delay action or greenwash unsustainable practices. Instruments such as transition bonds and performance-linked loans are increasingly being structured to tie financing terms to verifiable milestones.

Divestment strategies complement transition finance by signaling that certain activities are incompatible with a sustainable and regenerative future. Divestment typically involves withdrawing investments from industries such as coal mining, deforestation-linked agriculture, or companies with persistent records of human rights violations. It serves both ethical and financial purposes—limiting exposure to reputational and regulatory risks while sending a market signal about the future direction of capital flows.

Divestment decisions are often driven by fiduciary concerns as much as values. As climate risks become more visible and policy environments tighten, the long-term viability of carbon-intensive or socially harmful assets diminishes. Divestment campaigns, led by universities, pension funds, and faith-based organizations, have accelerated the normalization of fossil fuel divestment and spurred the development of climate-conscious investment products.

To avoid unintended consequences, divestment should be part of a broader capital reallocation strategy that supports reinvestment in regenerative sectors. Redirecting capital toward renewable energy, sustainable agriculture, circular infrastructure, and community development ensures that capital withdrawals are matched by constructive alternatives.

Engagement versus divestment is often debated. In some cases, continued investment combined with active shareholder engagement can be an effective tool for influencing corporate behavior. However, when dialogue fails to yield change or when core business models are fundamentally incompatible with a net positive trajectory, divestment becomes a necessary step.

Both transition financing and divestment strategies help reshape the financial system to support long-term sustainability and equity. When deployed together—with clarity, integrity, and purpose—they enable a managed shift away from harmful practices and toward regenerative, inclusive economic activity.

Net Positive Banking and Credit Models

As the financial system evolves to support the Net Positive Economy, banks and credit institutions are rethinking their role—not only as intermediaries of capital but as active enablers of regenerative and inclusive growth. Net positive banking and credit models are emerging as frameworks through which financial services can contribute more to environmental and social wellbeing than they extract or harm.

In a traditional banking model, credit is assessed primarily through risk and return considerations, often based on short-term financial metrics. Environmental and social externalities are typically not accounted for unless they pose reputational or regulatory risks. A net positive approach, by contrast, integrates sustainability into core banking functions—such as lending, investment, and advisory services—by aligning them with broader system outcomes.

Net positive banks set strategic goals that go beyond minimizing harm. This might include committing to finance more renewable energy than fossil fuels, supporting more nature-restoring activities than those that degrade ecosystems, or channeling more credit to underserved communities than they take from them. These commitments are operationalized through targeted lending criteria, sector exclusions, thematic products, and stakeholder engagement.

Sustainability-linked credit products—such as green mortgages, regenerative agriculture loans, and inclusive microfinance—enable banks to support borrowers aligned with net positive outcomes. These products often include preferential terms based on performance indicators such as emissions reduction, water efficiency, biodiversity improvement, or job creation in marginalized regions. Loan structures may also include technical assistance or capacity-building components to ensure long-term success.

Credit allocation frameworks are shifting to include environmental and social risk assessments. For instance, banks are increasingly using climate scenario analysis, nature risk assessments, and ESG scoring to guide lending decisions. In a net positive model, these tools help identify projects and businesses that not only avoid harm but contribute positively to regeneration and inclusion.

Community-based banking models—such as credit unions, cooperative banks, and community development financial institutions—have long demonstrated the value of place-based finance. These institutions often prioritize local reinvestment, democratic governance, and long-term relationship banking. Incorporating net positive principles into these models strengthens their potential to deliver systemic value.

Large banks are also beginning to embed net positive approaches into their strategies. Some have adopted science-based targets for their financed emissions, committed to nature-positive financing pathways, or developed internal taxonomies to steer credit toward sustainable and just transition activities. These efforts reflect a growing recognition that banking's license to operate depends on its contribution to a stable climate, healthy ecosystems, and inclusive societies.

However, challenges remain. Regulatory frameworks, incentive structures, and accounting standards are still evolving to accommodate net positive ambitions. There is also a need for greater transparency and harmonization of sustainability performance metrics across the sector.

Net positive banking is not simply about new products—it represents a shift in purpose. It asks financial institutions to assess how their operations impact people and the planet, and to use their influence to drive systemic change. By embedding regeneration and inclusion into their core business models, banks and credit providers can help finance a just and sustainable future.

Chapter 6: Innovation, Technology, and Data

This chapter explores how innovation and digital technologies can accelerate progress toward net positive outcomes. It covers the use of AI, IoT, blockchain, and predictive analytics in tracking and scaling impact. The chapter also examines pathways for regenerative design, smart infrastructure, and data-driven decision-making. Ethical considerations, access, and equity are discussed in the context of responsible innovation and the role of open data in supporting transparency.

Leveraging AI, IoT, and Blockchain to Track and Drive Net Positive Impact

Digital technologies are playing an increasingly important role in supporting the transition to a Net Positive Economy. Among the most promising are Artificial Intelligence (AI), the Internet of Things (IoT), and blockchain, which together offer powerful tools to measure, verify, and scale environmental and social impact. When deployed responsibly, these technologies can enhance transparency, efficiency, and accountability—core pillars of net positive strategies.

AI enables the analysis of vast and complex datasets to identify patterns, predict outcomes, and optimize decision-making. In the environmental domain, AI can be used to forecast climate risks, optimize renewable energy systems, track biodiversity changes, and improve resource use in agriculture and manufacturing. For example, AI algorithms can monitor satellite imagery to detect illegal deforestation or predict areas of water stress. In the social sphere, AI can help detect labor violations through anomaly detection in worker behavior data or support targeted interventions in underserved communities.

The IoT refers to networks of connected sensors and devices that collect and transmit real-time data. IoT technologies are being used to monitor air and water quality, track energy and water consumption, detect leaks, and optimize logistics and waste management. In agriculture, IoT can support precision farming, helping farmers reduce inputs and improve yields while minimizing environmental impact. These applications make it possible to monitor progress toward net positive goals on a continuous and localized basis.

Blockchain technology adds a layer of trust and traceability to impact reporting. Its decentralized ledger system ensures that data cannot be easily altered or manipulated, making it well-suited for verifying claims related to sustainable sourcing, carbon offsets, or financial flows. For instance, blockchain can trace the origin of materials in a supply chain, ensuring compliance with ethical and environmental standards. It can also track the distribution of ecosystem service payments, ensuring they reach intended beneficiaries.

When integrated, AI, IoT, and blockchain can create end-to-end systems that collect, analyze, and verify impact data across operations, supply chains, and portfolios. These systems support dynamic reporting, real-time decision-making, and adaptive management—critical features in the complex, rapidly changing environments where net positive strategies are deployed.

However, leveraging these technologies requires attention to governance, ethics, and access. Data privacy, algorithmic bias, and digital inequality are legitimate concerns that must be addressed to ensure that benefits are distributed fairly. Additionally, technology deployment must consider environmental impacts such as energy consumption, particularly in blockchain applications.

To maximize their value, organizations must invest in digital infrastructure, build internal capacity, and foster partnerships across sectors. When responsibly implemented, AI, IoT, and blockchain offer transformative potential to track progress, drive accountability, and scale positive outcomes in support of a Net Positive Economy.

Technological Pathways to Regenerative Design and Monitoring

Technology has become a central enabler in the shift toward regenerative economic systems. Beyond enhancing operational efficiency or reducing harm, emerging technologies are increasingly being used to design for regeneration, restore ecosystems, and monitor outcomes in ways that support the principles of a Net Positive Economy.

Regenerative design leverages technology to create systems—built environments, infrastructure, products, and processes—that contribute positively to ecological and social systems. This involves going beyond sustainability's focus on minimizing impact to designing for net ecological and human benefit. Technologies play a critical role in enabling such outcomes by providing the tools to simulate, model, and optimize regenerative performance from the outset.

In architecture and urban planning, for instance, parametric design tools and building information modeling (BIM) allow architects and engineers to assess how buildings interact with energy systems, water cycles, and ecosystems. These technologies help optimize building orientation, material use, green space integration, and passive climate control, making it possible to develop structures that produce more energy than they consume or enhance local biodiversity.

In agriculture and land management, geo-spatial mapping and remote sensing support the design of regenerative landscapes. By identifying soil types, hydrological patterns, and vegetation cover, planners can restore degraded lands with context-specific solutions. Drone technology allows for precision planting, monitoring of restoration progress, and early detection of erosion or invasive species.

In product design, life cycle analysis (LCA) tools help manufacturers evaluate environmental and social impacts across the entire life cycle of a product—from raw material extraction to end-of-life. These tools support decisions about materials, manufacturing processes, logistics, and recovery strategies. When integrated into early design stages, they enable regenerative product innovation—such as biodegradable packaging, recyclable electronics, or upcycled materials.

Monitoring and verification technologies are also critical. Regeneration is a process that unfolds over time and across multiple dimensions. Technologies such as satellite imaging, acoustic sensors, and machine learning algorithms allow for continuous monitoring of environmental indicators like forest cover, water quality, carbon fluxes, and species abundance. These systems can detect subtle changes in ecosystem health and help calibrate management interventions in near real-time.

Social monitoring tools, including mobile-based surveys and participatory data platforms, can be used to assess the impacts of regenerative projects on community wellbeing. These tools make it easier to include local voices in performance assessments and provide data that goes beyond standard economic indicators.

Crucially, regenerative design and monitoring technologies must be applied with attention to context, inclusivity, and transparency. Local knowledge should inform the interpretation of data and the design of interventions. Open data systems and inclusive governance structures help ensure that technological tools support democratic decision-making and equitable benefit-sharing.

When integrated thoughtfully, technology becomes a catalyst for regenerative outcomes—enabling stakeholders to restore ecosystems, strengthen communities, and continuously improve the systems they rely on. In doing so, it reinforces the foundational goals of the Net Positive Economy.

Digital Twins, Remote Sensing, and Predictive Analytics

Advanced technologies such as digital twins, remote sensing, and predictive analytics are reshaping how organizations model, understand, and manage their environmental and social impacts. These tools offer powerful capabilities to simulate scenarios, monitor complex systems, and anticipate future conditions—making them especially valuable in the pursuit of net positive outcomes.

Digital twins are virtual representations of physical systems—such as buildings, factories, cities, or ecosystems—that are continuously updated with real-time data. By integrating inputs from sensors, IoT devices, and environmental monitoring platforms, digital twins enable users to visualize how systems behave under different conditions. In a net positive context, they can be used to test the impact of design choices, track performance against regenerative goals, and inform adaptive management.

For example, a digital twin of a watershed can simulate how different land-use practices affect water flows, biodiversity, and sedimentation. In urban planning, digital twins of buildings or districts can model energy use, carbon emissions, and heat island effects, helping cities plan for greater sustainability and resilience. The use of digital twins supports proactive decision-making and reduces the risk of unintended consequences by providing a more complete understanding of system dynamics.

Remote sensing involves the use of satellite imagery, aerial drones, and ground-based sensors to monitor environmental and land-use changes. These technologies provide large-scale, high-resolution data on variables such as vegetation cover, soil moisture, land degradation, deforestation, and urban sprawl. Remote sensing plays a critical role in tracking the progress of regenerative projects, assessing ecosystem health, and identifying areas for intervention.

In agriculture, remote sensing supports precision land management by providing information on crop health, irrigation needs, and pest outbreaks. In conservation, it helps detect illegal logging or mining activities in real time. Combined with machine learning, remote sensing data can be rapidly processed to produce insights that inform both local actions and broader policy decisions.

Predictive analytics uses historical and real-time data to forecast future outcomes. These tools are increasingly being applied to model the impacts of climate change, resource depletion, or demographic shifts. For businesses and governments aiming for net positive strategies, predictive analytics can help anticipate where risks will emerge, where opportunities for regeneration exist, and what the long-term implications of different policy or investment choices may be.

For instance, predictive models can assess how different carbon reduction pathways align with global climate targets or forecast the resilience of supply chains under various environmental scenarios. In community development, these tools can be used to anticipate service needs, infrastructure demand, or social vulnerabilities.

The integration of these technologies supports a more intelligent, responsive, and evidence-based approach to sustainability. However, their effectiveness depends on data quality, cross-sector collaboration, and ethical governance. Ensuring that models are transparent, inclusive, and regularly validated is essential to maintaining trust and accountability.

Together, digital twins, remote sensing, and predictive analytics provide organizations with a powerful set of tools to plan, manage, and scale regenerative initiatives. Their use marks a shift from reactive to proactive sustainability—one that anticipates challenges, informs solutions, and reinforces the core objectives of the Net Positive Economy.

Scaling Innovations in Clean Tech, Regenerative Agriculture, and Smart Infrastructure

Scaling innovation across key sectors is essential for realizing the goals of a Net Positive Economy. While many regenerative technologies and practices already exist, their adoption remains uneven due to financial, regulatory, and institutional barriers. Accelerating uptake in areas such as clean technology, regenerative agriculture, and smart infrastructure offers significant potential to drive environmental restoration, enhance resilience, and generate inclusive economic opportunities.

Clean technology (clean tech) refers to innovations that reduce negative environmental impacts through renewable energy, energy efficiency, and resource optimization. Solar photovoltaics, wind turbines, battery storage, green hydrogen, and electrification technologies are core components of the global transition away from fossil fuels. The net positive approach supports not only the deployment of clean tech but its integration into systems that actively improve environmental conditions—such as buildings that generate surplus energy or grids that optimize for renewable inputs and load balancing.

Scaling clean tech requires supportive policies, financing mechanisms, and infrastructure. Feed-in tariffs, tax incentives, and green procurement policies can stimulate demand, while blended finance and concessional lending can de-risk investment in emerging technologies. Local manufacturing and workforce development are also critical to ensuring that clean tech expansion supports inclusive job creation.

Regenerative agriculture involves practices that restore soil health, enhance biodiversity, and improve water retention while maintaining or increasing yields. Techniques such as no-till farming, cover cropping, agroforestry, rotational grazing, and compost application build natural capital and reduce dependence on synthetic inputs.

These approaches sequester carbon, support pollinator habitats, and enhance ecosystem resilience.

To scale regenerative agriculture, technical training, market access, and incentives must be aligned. Governments can reform subsidies to reward outcomes rather than inputs, and private sector actors can support transition finance, supply chain traceability, and fair pricing for regenerative products. Peer-to-peer learning networks and demonstration farms can also help accelerate adoption and innovation at the local level.

Smart infrastructure integrates digital technologies with physical systems to improve performance, reduce emissions, and respond adaptively to environmental and social needs. Examples include smart water networks that detect leaks and optimize flows, energy-efficient buildings with dynamic controls, and public transportation systems enhanced by real-time data. In a net positive framework, smart infrastructure supports not only efficiency but regeneration—for instance, using permeable surfaces to recharge aquifers or integrating green roofs to improve air quality and biodiversity.

Scaling smart infrastructure involves cross-sector collaboration among planners, engineers, utilities, and technology providers. It also requires investment in digital infrastructure, data governance frameworks, and long-term maintenance strategies. Community involvement in design and deployment ensures that smart systems reflect local priorities and enhance quality of life.

Across all three domains, scaling innovation must be accompanied by inclusive governance, capacity-building, and equitable access to technology. Without attention to these factors, benefits may be unevenly distributed, or adoption may reinforce existing inequalities.

When clean tech, regenerative agriculture, and smart infrastructure are deployed at scale with integrity and coordination, they become foundational drivers of systemic transformation. Their expansion is not only a technological task but a societal one—requiring alignment across institutions, stakeholders, and geographies to deliver on the promise of the Net Positive Economy.

Ethics, Access, and Equity in Net Positive Innovation

As innovation becomes a cornerstone of the Net Positive Economy, ensuring that technological development and deployment align with ethical standards, universal access, and social equity is essential. Without these safeguards, well-intentioned innovations can unintentionally reinforce inequalities, marginalize vulnerable populations, or cause environmental harm. A net positive approach therefore embeds ethics and inclusion into every stage of the innovation process—from design and funding to scaling and impact evaluation.

Ethics in innovation begins with purpose. Technologies developed to support net positive goals must be designed not only for performance or efficiency but also for integrity, safety, and responsible use. This includes anticipating unintended consequences, ensuring data privacy, avoiding environmental trade-offs, and respecting cultural and community norms. Ethical innovation frameworks—such as responsible AI principles or bioethics protocols—provide guidance for developers, funders, and regulators in identifying and managing potential risks.

Access to innovation is another critical consideration. Many regenerative and low-carbon technologies remain out of reach for lower-income communities, small businesses, and countries in the Global South due to high costs, weak infrastructure, or restrictive intellectual property regimes. Net positive innovation requires addressing these barriers through inclusive design, open-source licensing, affordable financing models, and targeted policy support. Innovations must be scalable not only technologically, but socially and economically as well.

Equity also involves addressing representation and participation in the innovation process. Diverse perspectives—across gender, race, age, geography, and expertise—help ensure that innovations respond to a wide range of needs and realities. Participatory innovation approaches, such as co-design or community-driven research, enable users and affected groups to shape technologies and ensure they reflect lived experiences. This fosters legitimacy, adoption, and greater alignment with local priorities.

Digital inequality remains a barrier to equitable access. Many regenerative innovations rely on connectivity, data literacy, and digital infrastructure. Closing the digital divide—through expanded broadband access, affordable devices, and digital skills training—is a prerequisite for inclusive participation in the net positive transition. Public-private partnerships and targeted investment can help ensure that innovation ecosystems do not exclude those most in need of solutions.

Moreover, equity must extend across value chains. Workers in innovation-intensive sectors—such as clean energy, tech manufacturing, or agriculture—must benefit from fair wages, safe working conditions, and career development opportunities. Ensuring that the social benefits of innovation are distributed throughout the production and delivery process reinforces long-term resilience and public support.

Finally, accountability mechanisms are essential to assess whether innovation is delivering net positive outcomes. Impact assessments should include social and ethical dimensions, and governance structures should enable redress or course correction when technologies fail to meet intended goals. Transparency in reporting and inclusive stakeholder feedback loops help maintain trust and continuous improvement.

Innovation that ignores ethics, access, and equity may deliver efficiency gains but will fall short of transformative potential. In contrast, innovation that centers these principles contributes not only to regenerative environmental outcomes but to a more just and inclusive economy. Embedding these values from the outset ensures that the benefits of a Net Positive Economy are widely shared and durable.

Open Data and Digital Transparency

In a Net Positive Economy, access to information is a public good that supports accountability, trust, and collaboration. Open data and digital transparency are therefore essential enablers of regenerative and inclusive systems. They provide stakeholders with the tools to track progress, evaluate claims, and participate meaningfully in decision-making processes.

Open data refers to data that is made freely available for anyone to access, use, and share—typically under non-restrictive licenses. In the sustainability context, this can include emissions inventories, land use data, biodiversity records, water quality monitoring, and supply chain disclosures. When standardized and made accessible, such data supports scientific research, policy development, investment decisions, and civic engagement.

Digital transparency extends beyond data access to include how information is collected, processed, interpreted, and communicated. Transparent algorithms, modeling assumptions, and performance metrics are crucial for ensuring that stakeholders can understand and evaluate the basis of decisions and claims—especially those related to net positive outcomes. This is particularly important in the age of artificial intelligence and predictive analytics, where opaque systems may obscure important trade-offs or biases.

For businesses and investors, open data and transparency enhance credibility and stakeholder trust. Publicly reporting environmental and social performance, including progress toward net positive targets, allows customers, regulators, and civil society to independently verify claims. Transparency can also strengthen market positioning, attract impact-oriented capital, and support alignment with voluntary standards and frameworks such as the TCFD or the GRI.

For governments, making data available and usable enables cross-sector collaboration and more effective public policy. Shared data platforms can support regional sustainability planning, emergency response coordination, or infrastructure investment strategies. They also enable benchmarking and comparative performance analysis across jurisdictions.

Technology plays a key role in facilitating open data. Cloud-based platforms, APIs (application programming interfaces), data visualization tools, and geospatial dashboards make it easier for users to find, interpret, and act on information. Open-source software and interoperable data formats increase usability across systems and organizations. However, technical capacity, digital literacy, and inclusive design remain important for ensuring equitable access and avoiding unintended exclusion.

At the same time, open data systems must address privacy, security, and consent—especially when dealing with community-generated, personal, or culturally sensitive information. Governance frameworks that balance transparency with rights protections are essential for maintaining legitimacy and ethical integrity.

Finally, open data supports collaborative problem-solving. Researchers, entrepreneurs, civil society organizations, and communities can co-create solutions when they have access to timely and relevant data. This accelerates innovation, identifies opportunities for regeneration, and fosters collective action toward shared goals.

In sum, open data and digital transparency are not peripheral to the Net Positive Economy—they are foundational. By making impact information accessible, credible, and actionable, they create the conditions for systems change grounded in evidence, participation, and accountability.

Chapter 7: Governance, Policy, and Institutional Change

This chapter focuses on the governance and policy environment required to enable net positive transitions. It reviews the role of public institutions, multi-level governance structures, and legal innovations such as rights of nature and ESG mandates. Key policy tools—including carbon pricing, standards, and taxation—are discussed in relation to both risk and opportunity. The chapter emphasizes coordination across sectors and scales to ensure coherent, forward-looking policy frameworks.

Role of Public Institutions in Enabling Net Positive Transitions

Public institutions play a foundational role in shaping the enabling environment for a Net Positive Economy. Through laws, regulations, investment, and coordination, governments and public agencies establish the incentives, safeguards, and frameworks that guide how economies function. As such, their involvement is essential in scaling regenerative and inclusive practices beyond isolated initiatives into systemic transformation.

At the national level, governments influence market behavior through fiscal and regulatory policy. They can promote net positive transitions by enacting legislation that sets minimum sustainability standards, such as emissions limits, biodiversity protection, or labor rights. They can also provide public investments in infrastructure and research and development that support regeneration—such as nature-based solutions, clean energy grids, or public transit systems.

Public procurement is another powerful lever. As major buyers of goods and services, governments can prioritize suppliers that demonstrate net positive performance. This sends strong market signals, de-risks early adoption, and stimulates demand for sustainable and inclusive innovation. Policies that integrate life-cycle thinking into procurement decisions help ensure that public spending delivers environmental and social co-benefits.

Subnational governments—cities, regions, and municipalities—also have a critical role, especially in implementing place-based solutions. Urban planning, land use regulation, water management, and building codes all fall under local jurisdiction in many countries. By embedding net positive principles into these domains, local authorities can drive integrated approaches that reflect local needs and contexts.

Public financial institutions, such as development banks and sovereign wealth funds, influence capital flows by providing concessional finance, guarantees, or equity to projects aligned with national and international sustainability goals. Their ability to take on risk and catalyze private investment makes them key players in emerging sectors such as regenerative agriculture, circular economy, and ecosystem restoration.

Institutional mandates are evolving in response to global frameworks like the Paris Agreement and the Kunming-Montreal Global Biodiversity Framework. Increasingly, public institutions are expected not just to mitigate harm but to contribute positively to climate resilience, ecosystem health, and social inclusion. This is reflected in updated national development plans, climate adaptation strategies, and sustainability-linked public budgets.

Coordination across ministries and sectors is essential to align economic, environmental, and social policies. Cross-cutting governance mechanisms—such as national sustainability councils, inter-ministerial task forces, or multi-stakeholder commissions—can help bridge policy silos and ensure coherence across energy, agriculture, industry, finance, and social protection agendas.

Finally, public institutions must lead by example. Greening public buildings, electrifying fleets, adopting inclusive hiring practices, and ensuring transparency in operations reinforce the credibility of government commitments and demonstrate what is possible in practice.

In enabling net positive transitions, public institutions are not simply regulators or funders—they are architects of long-term societal pathways. Their ability to foster stability, mobilize resources, and convene diverse actors makes them uniquely positioned to drive the systems change required for a regenerative and inclusive future.

Policy Tools: Carbon Pricing, Incentives, Standards, and Taxation

To support the transition to a Net Positive Economy, governments deploy a range of policy tools that influence behavior, reshape markets, and reallocate resources. Among the most effective are carbon pricing mechanisms, targeted incentives, regulatory standards, and taxation policies—each playing a distinct but complementary role in aligning economic activity with environmental regeneration and social inclusion.

Carbon pricing—through carbon taxes or emissions trading schemes (ETS)—assigns a cost to greenhouse gas emissions, internalizing climate-related externalities into market decisions. By increasing the cost of carbon-intensive activities, carbon pricing encourages investment in cleaner alternatives and generates public revenue that can be reinvested in climate adaptation, social equity measures, or low-carbon infrastructure. For carbon pricing to support net positive outcomes, it must be science-aligned, predictable, and designed to avoid regressive impacts on vulnerable populations.

Incentives encourage desirable behavior by lowering the cost of sustainable practices or enhancing the return on regenerative investment. These can take the form of subsidies, tax credits, grants, loan guarantees, or accelerated depreciation for assets such as renewable energy systems, soil restoration projects, circular manufacturing, or sustainable buildings. Incentive schemes help de-risk early adoption, support market development, and signal policy intent. However, they must be carefully designed to avoid unintended consequences, such as over-subsidizing mature technologies or supporting marginal improvements that fall short of regenerative goals.

Regulatory standards establish clear rules and minimum performance thresholds for industries, products, and services. These include environmental standards (e.g., air and water quality), building codes, emissions limits, product durability requirements, and disclosure obligations. In a net positive context, standards are evolving to include positive performance criteria—for example, mandating biodiversity gain in new developments or requiring companies to demonstrate nature-based contributions. Standards provide clarity, level the playing field, and can drive innovation by setting ambitious but achievable targets.

Taxation policy influences production and consumption patterns by adjusting price signals. Environmental taxes—such as those on resource extraction, waste generation, or pollution—discourage harmful practices and generate revenue that can be recycled into sustainable initiatives. At the same time, tax relief can be offered for activities that restore ecosystems, reduce inequality, or support community resilience. In many jurisdictions, reforming environmentally harmful subsidies (e.g., for fossil fuels or industrial agriculture) is a prerequisite for effective green taxation.

The effectiveness of these tools depends on context, coherence, and credibility. Policies must be tailored to local economic structures, institutional capacities, and social conditions. They should also be integrated across ministries and policy areas to avoid conflicting signals or duplication. Transparency in policy design and implementation builds stakeholder trust and enhances compliance.

Moreover, policy instruments should be adaptive—able to evolve based on performance data, technological advancements, and shifting societal expectations. Periodic review processes and stakeholder consultation mechanisms help maintain policy relevance and effectiveness.

When deployed strategically, carbon pricing, incentives, standards, and taxation create a policy environment that rewards regeneration, penalizes degradation, and supports inclusive growth. Together, these tools form the backbone of a policy architecture capable of steering economies toward net positive outcomes.

International Cooperation and Trade in a Regenerative Economy

Global challenges such as climate change, biodiversity loss, and inequality transcend national borders. As a result, the transition to a Net Positive Economy cannot be achieved in isolation—it requires robust and sustained international cooperation, particularly in areas like trade, finance, technology transfer, and environmental governance. A regenerative global economy depends on countries working together to align rules, incentives, and practices in support of shared ecological and social goals.

International trade plays a central role in shaping patterns of production and consumption. Trade agreements influence how natural resources are managed, how emissions are accounted for, and how value is distributed across supply chains. To support regenerative outcomes, trade frameworks must evolve to promote sustainable production practices, ensure fair labor conditions, and recognize environmental externalities.

This includes incorporating sustainability standards and environmental provisions into trade agreements—such as commitments to eliminate deforestation-linked commodities, reduce carbon intensity, or uphold international labor rights. Such provisions can help create a level playing field and prevent a "race to the bottom" in environmental or social protections. However, they must be designed carefully to avoid protectionism or unintended barriers for developing countries.

Technology transfer and capacity building are vital components of international cooperation. Many countries in the Global South face constraints in accessing the knowledge, tools, and finance needed to implement net positive strategies. Mechanisms such as international climate finance, intellectual property waivers, and technical assistance programs help bridge this gap and enable equitable participation in the regenerative transition. Ensuring that technology transfer is inclusive, context-sensitive, and responsive to local priorities enhances its long-term effectiveness.

Climate diplomacy and multilateral environmental agreements also play a critical role. Frameworks such as the Paris Agreement, the Convention on Biological Diversity, and the Sustainable Development Goals create common objectives and accountability structures. By committing to shared targets—such as limiting warming to 1.5°C or protecting 30% of land and oceans—countries signal their intent to align domestic policies with global sustainability goals.

Border adjustment mechanisms, such as carbon border taxes, are emerging tools to prevent carbon leakage and encourage global alignment on emissions reduction. While these policies aim to ensure that environmental regulations are not undermined by international competition, they must be carefully implemented to account for developmental differences and avoid reinforcing global inequality.

Financial cooperation—through multilateral development banks, green bond standards, and blended finance platforms—facilitates cross-border investment in regenerative infrastructure, ecosystem restoration, and social inclusion. Coordinated efforts in setting global taxonomies and ESG disclosure standards also help ensure consistency and comparability in sustainability performance across markets.

Ultimately, international cooperation in a regenerative economy must be grounded in equity, solidarity, and mutual benefit. Developed countries have a responsibility to lead on emissions reductions, provide financial support, and address historical imbalances in trade and development. Meanwhile, developing countries must be empowered to define their own pathways to regeneration and resilience.

A Net Positive Economy thrives when cooperation is based on shared purpose and collective action. Strengthening international collaboration across trade, finance, and governance is essential for ensuring that regeneration and inclusion become defining features of the global economy.

Multi-Level Governance from Local to Global

The transition to a Net Positive Economy involves complex interactions across scales—from households and municipalities to national governments and international bodies. Effective multi-level governance ensures that policies and actions at each level are coherent, complementary, and aligned with broader sustainability objectives. It facilitates collaboration, minimizes policy gaps, and enables solutions tailored to diverse geographic, cultural, and economic contexts.

At the local level, governments and community institutions are often closest to implementation. They oversee land-use planning, water management, housing, transport, and social services—domains central to regenerative and inclusive development. Local actors can also mobilize community knowledge, foster stakeholder engagement, and pilot innovative approaches that reflect specific ecological and social realities. Their ability to build trust and legitimacy makes them essential partners in translating national strategies into tangible outcomes.

Regional and provincial authorities serve as critical intermediaries. They coordinate across municipalities, manage shared natural resources, and implement infrastructure projects that span jurisdictions. In some contexts, they also hold legislative authority over key areas such as agriculture, energy, or education. Aligning regional development plans with net positive goals helps ensure that subnational investments contribute to national and global targets.

National governments remain central to enabling multi-level governance. They provide legal frameworks, fiscal transfers, regulatory guidance, and capacity-building support to lower levels of government. National planning processes—such as climate action plans, biodiversity strategies, or development blueprints—set the overall direction, but their success depends on alignment with subnational realities and priorities.

Vertical coordination is essential for policy coherence. Mechanisms such as intergovernmental councils, national-local dialogues, and joint task forces help synchronize objectives, share information, and manage trade-offs. For example, aligning national climate goals with urban development policies ensures that infrastructure investments reinforce emissions reduction and resilience objectives.

At the global level, multi-level governance is supported by international agreements and networks that connect actors across scales. These include UN frameworks, transnational city coalitions, regional development organizations, and global standard-setting bodies. They create shared benchmarks, foster learning, and promote accountability through peer review and voluntary reporting mechanisms.

Importantly, effective multi-level governance is not only about formal institutions—it also involves inclusive participation from civil society, Indigenous peoples, youth, and the private sector. Collaborative governance models—such as participatory budgeting, community benefit agreements, and multi-stakeholder partnerships—ensure that diverse voices shape decisions and outcomes.

Technology plays a growing role in enhancing coordination. Digital platforms for data sharing, real-time monitoring, and collaborative planning support transparency and alignment across levels.

However, capacity disparities—especially in under-resourced local governments—must be addressed to ensure equitable participation.

In sum, multi-level governance provides the connective tissue for a Net Positive Economy. It links top-down ambition with bottom-up action, promotes integrated solutions, and builds resilience across systems. Strengthening this coordination is key to managing complexity and driving systemic change in an inclusive and context-sensitive way.

Legal Innovations: Rights of Nature, ESG Disclosure Mandates

Legal frameworks are evolving to meet the demands of a Net Positive Economy. In recent years, a wave of legal innovations has emerged to redefine the relationship between human systems, the environment, and corporate responsibility. Notable developments include the recognition of the rights of nature and the introduction of mandatory ESG disclosure requirements—both of which aim to embed regenerative and inclusive principles into law.

The rights of nature is a legal concept that recognizes ecosystems—such as rivers, forests, and mountains—as legal entities with rights to exist, thrive, and evolve. This approach challenges the traditional view of nature as property and instead treats it as a subject of law, entitled to protection. Countries such as Ecuador, New Zealand, Colombia, and parts of the United States and India have adopted various forms of this legal innovation.

By granting legal standing to ecosystems, rights of nature frameworks allow individuals or communities to act on their behalf in court, creating new avenues for environmental protection and ecological restoration. These frameworks shift legal systems toward recognizing the intrinsic value of nature, beyond its utility to humans, and support a paradigm where economic activity must operate within ecological boundaries.

For the Net Positive Economy, rights of nature laws provide a foundation for aligning development with planetary health. They reinforce the principle that regeneration should not be optional or voluntary but an obligation embedded in governance. Moreover, they encourage new forms of co-governance involving Indigenous peoples, civil society, and public agencies.

In parallel, mandatory ESG disclosure requirements are transforming how companies report and manage their environmental and social impacts. These legal mandates compel organizations—especially large firms and financial institutions—to disclose information on issues such as climate risk, emissions, water use, biodiversity impacts, labor practices, and board diversity. Emerging regulations in jurisdictions like the European Union (e.g., the Corporate Sustainability Reporting Directive), the United Kingdom, and the United States are setting new standards for disclosure quality, scope, and verification.

These mandates are grounded in the principle that transparency is essential for accountability and market efficiency. They help investors assess non-financial risks, allow regulators to track progress toward national goals, and enable the public to understand how companies are contributing to—or undermining—sustainability outcomes.

For disclosures to support net positive objectives, they must go beyond compliance checklists and focus on meaningful performance metrics. This includes reporting on contributions to regeneration (e.g., carbon sequestration, habitat restoration) and inclusion (e.g., equity in hiring, supplier diversity), alongside conventional risk indicators.

Legal innovations such as these signal a shift toward a more expansive and systemic understanding of rights, responsibilities, and impacts. They enable courts, regulators, and citizens to hold actors accountable for environmental and social outcomes and create a legal architecture that supports transformation.

As legal systems continue to evolve, aligning laws with net positive values—ecological restoration, intergenerational equity, and inclusive prosperity—will be central to institutionalizing long-term sustainability across sectors and geographies.

Regulatory Risk and Opportunity in a Net Positive Policy Framework

As governments strengthen environmental and social regulations in response to global challenges, organizations face an evolving landscape of regulatory risks—but also significant opportunities. In a Net Positive Economy, regulation is not merely a constraint to be managed; it becomes a tool for transformation, innovation, and value creation.

Regulatory risk typically refers to the potential financial or operational impacts resulting from new laws, shifting compliance requirements, or stricter enforcement. For companies with high environmental footprints or poor social performance, this risk is growing. New regulations—such as carbon pricing, extended producer responsibility, mandatory ESG disclosures, and bans on harmful substances—can lead to increased costs, legal liabilities, or loss of market access.

For example, companies that rely on fossil fuels or single-use plastics may face higher taxation or restrictions. Firms with opaque supply chains could be exposed to penalties under due diligence laws targeting deforestation, forced labor, or biodiversity loss. Reputational risk may also rise if companies are perceived as lagging behind regulatory expectations or failing to meet stakeholder demands for transparency and accountability.

However, this same regulatory evolution creates opportunities for forward-thinking organizations. Firms that anticipate and align with emerging policy frameworks can gain a competitive advantage—by accessing incentives, attracting impact-oriented investors, and meeting consumer preferences for ethical and sustainable products.

Compliance becomes a foundation for leadership, innovation, and trust-building.

Regulation can also serve as a market-shaping mechanism, creating demand for sustainable technologies, products, and services. For instance, building performance standards drive the adoption of energy-efficient materials and smart infrastructure. Circular economy regulations support markets for recycled materials, repair services, and product-as-a-service models. In these cases, regulation levels the playing field and accelerates business models aligned with net positive principles.

Policy certainty and clarity are key to unlocking opportunity. When rules are consistent, science-based, and developed through stakeholder engagement, they reduce uncertainty and encourage long-term investment. Companies can plan transitions, build capacity, and innovate with greater confidence when regulatory pathways are predictable and aligned with international commitments such as the Paris Agreement or the Sustainable Development Goals.

Engagement with regulators is also part of effective risk and opportunity management. Companies that participate in public consultations, share data, and co-develop standards can help shape pragmatic policies that balance ambition with feasibility. Collaborative regulation, where public and private actors work together to develop solutions, is increasingly used to address complex sustainability issues.

Finally, organizations must build internal capacity to navigate the changing regulatory environment. This includes horizon scanning, policy scenario analysis, and integrating regulatory considerations into strategy, governance, and reporting systems. Strengthening legal, compliance, and sustainability functions ensures that businesses remain agile and resilient in the face of policy shifts.

In the context of a Net Positive Economy, regulation is not just about avoiding penalties—it's about enabling transformation. Companies that align their strategies with emerging policy trends can reduce risk, capture new value, and contribute to a global economic system that restores, rather than depletes, environmental and social capital.

Chapter 8: Corporate Leadership and Strategic Integration

This chapter addresses how businesses can embed net positive goals into their vision, strategy, and operations. It highlights the importance of executive leadership, board accountability, and organizational culture in driving change. Topics include transitioning legacy systems, aligning supply chains with regenerative goals, and fostering stakeholder engagement. The chapter presents strategic pathways for integrating sustainability into core business functions.

Embedding Net Positive Goals in Corporate Vision and Strategy

Achieving a Net Positive Economy requires that businesses not only adopt sustainability practices but fully integrate net positive goals into their core vision and strategic decision-making. This integration goes beyond incremental improvements to represent a shift in how organizations define success, allocate resources, and engage with stakeholders.

A corporate vision grounded in net positive thinking articulates a purpose that extends beyond financial performance to include measurable contributions to environmental regeneration and social wellbeing. Rather than positioning sustainability as a risk to be managed or a peripheral initiative, this vision embeds it at the heart of value creation. It signals to employees, investors, customers, and partners that the company is committed to leaving the world better than it found it.

Translating this vision into strategy requires a clear articulation of long-term goals, aligned with planetary boundaries and social foundations. These may include objectives such as becoming nature-positive, water-positive, carbon-negative, or equity-enhancing. Setting these ambitions publicly—and linking them to science-based targets—helps ensure accountability and internal alignment.

Strategic integration involves evaluating all major decisions—investments, product development, acquisitions, and operations—through a net positive lens. This may require adopting new planning tools, impact assessment methodologies, or sustainability criteria for capital expenditure. For example, a company might apply a "net impact screen" to prioritize initiatives that deliver positive outcomes across environmental and social domains, not just those that minimize harm.

Embedding net positive thinking also involves reimagining business models. For product-based companies, this could mean shifting from linear production to circular service models. For extractive industries, it might involve investing in ecosystem restoration and local community ownership. Financial firms may realign portfolios to favor regenerative investments, while tech firms can prioritize digital inclusion and energy efficiency.

Organizational structure and incentives must support this shift. Sustainability and impact performance should be integrated into business units, with clear accountability at the executive and board levels. Performance evaluations, bonuses, and promotion pathways should reflect contributions to net positive goals alongside traditional financial metrics.

Internal communication and culture play a key role. Employees need to understand the company's vision and how their roles contribute to broader impact. Purpose-led storytelling, employee engagement programs, and ongoing training can help build a shared sense of responsibility and motivation across the organization.

External stakeholders—including investors, regulators, customers, and civil society—expect transparency and consistency in how net positive strategies are developed and implemented. Regular reporting, third-party assurance, and participation in industry initiatives enhance credibility and facilitate benchmarking.

Ultimately, embedding net positive goals into corporate vision and strategy positions companies to thrive in a world increasingly shaped by environmental limits and social expectations. It turns sustainability from a constraint into a source of innovation, differentiation, and long-term value creation.

Beyond Compliance: Purpose-Driven Business Models

In a Net Positive Economy, companies are expected to move beyond compliance with environmental and social regulations and adopt purpose-driven business models that create positive value for both society and the planet. This shift reflects a growing recognition that traditional compliance-based approaches—while important—are not sufficient to address the scale and urgency of global challenges.

Compliance models tend to focus on meeting minimum legal standards and avoiding penalties. They are reactive, risk-averse, and typically driven by external pressure rather than internal ambition. While such models have contributed to improvements in environmental performance and corporate governance, they often fall short in catalyzing the kind of transformative change needed for regeneration and inclusion.

Purpose-driven business models, by contrast, are proactive and impact-oriented. They are built around a clear social or environmental mission that informs how the business operates, what it offers, and how it measures success. These models are not limited to social enterprises or B Corps; increasingly, mainstream companies are redefining their purpose to align with stakeholder expectations and global sustainability goals.

A purpose-driven business begins with a core question: What positive role can this organization play in society and the environment? The answer shapes everything from product design and sourcing to workforce practices and financial strategies. For example, a construction firm may reorient its model around building climate-resilient infrastructure that restores ecosystems. A consumer goods company may commit to eliminating waste across its value chain and supporting community livelihoods through inclusive procurement.

These models often integrate shared value approaches, where solving social or environmental problems also unlocks business opportunity. For instance, investing in regenerative agriculture may reduce supply chain risk while enhancing brand credibility and consumer trust. Similarly, expanding access to clean energy in underserved markets can generate new revenue streams while contributing to development goals.

Innovation is a key driver of purpose-driven models. Companies invest in research and development not only to improve efficiency or reduce costs but to create new solutions with regenerative potential. This might include biodegradable materials, modular product systems, or digital tools that promote transparency and ethical sourcing.

Governance structures must support this orientation. Purpose needs to be embedded in decision-making frameworks, accountability systems, and corporate governance. Some companies formalize their purpose through legal structures, such as benefit corporations, or by adopting purpose clauses in their articles of incorporation.

Stakeholder engagement is central. Purpose-driven firms actively listen to and collaborate with customers, employees, communities, and partners to co-create value. This relational approach strengthens trust and helps ensure that strategies are relevant, inclusive, and grounded in real-world needs.

Importantly, purpose-driven business models are not static. They evolve based on learning, feedback, and changing societal expectations. Companies must remain agile and open to transformation as they deepen their commitment to regeneration and equity.

By going beyond compliance, businesses position themselves not just as followers of regulation but as leaders of systemic change. Purpose-driven models offer a compelling pathway to resilience, relevance, and positive impact in the transition to a Net Positive Economy.

Supply Chain Regeneration and End-to-End Value Alignment

In a Net Positive Economy, organizations are increasingly expected to take responsibility not only for their direct operations but also for the broader systems in which they operate—most notably, their supply chains. A truly net positive approach requires supply chain regeneration and full end-to-end value alignment, ensuring that positive environmental and social impacts are delivered at every stage of production and delivery.

Traditional supply chains often rely on linear, extractive models that externalize costs—such as ecosystem degradation, low wages, or unsafe working conditions—while focusing narrowly on price, speed, and efficiency. This approach undermines long-term resilience and misses opportunities for collaborative innovation, trust-building, and systemic improvement.

Supply chain regeneration involves redesigning sourcing, production, and distribution processes to restore natural systems, empower local communities, and create shared value. This includes shifting from monoculture-based agricultural inputs to regenerative farming practices, restoring forest ecosystems along commodity chains, or supporting biodiversity in fisheries and aquaculture. It may also involve working with smallholder farmers or local producers to increase soil health, reduce chemical inputs, and improve livelihoods.

Regenerative supply chains require traceability and transparency. Organizations must be able to map and monitor their suppliers—sometimes through multiple tiers—to assess risks and opportunities for positive impact. Technologies such as blockchain, remote sensing, and AI-assisted supply chain analytics help track sourcing origins, compliance with sustainability standards, and real-time changes in environmental or social conditions.

Achieving end-to-end value alignment means that each actor in the value chain—from raw material supplier to end consumer—is guided by shared principles of regeneration, inclusion, and long-term value creation. This involves rethinking procurement practices to prioritize sustainability, creating incentives for suppliers to invest in sustainable practices, and designing performance metrics that go beyond price and delivery timelines.

Contracts and purchasing agreements can be restructured to reflect shared net positive goals. For instance, long-term contracts that include environmental or social performance clauses can provide suppliers with the security needed to make transformative investments. Capacity-building initiatives, co-financing models, and knowledge-sharing platforms can also support suppliers—particularly small and medium-sized enterprises—in adopting regenerative practices.

Collaboration across sectors and competitors is often necessary to drive supply chain transformation. Pre-competitive partnerships allow companies to set common standards, invest jointly in infrastructure (such as sustainable logistics or processing facilities), and support collective impact initiatives. Industry platforms and multi-stakeholder coalitions are instrumental in advancing regenerative benchmarks and increasing alignment.

Consumer-facing brands have a unique opportunity—and responsibility—to communicate how supply chain practices reflect their values and commitments. Storytelling, labeling, and public reporting can increase consumer awareness and reward regenerative choices. However, such communications must be evidence-based and free from greenwashing.

By focusing on supply chain regeneration and end-to-end value alignment, organizations can amplify their net positive impact well beyond their operational boundaries. In doing so, they strengthen resilience, build stakeholder trust, and help shift entire industries toward a regenerative and inclusive future.

Executive Leadership, Board Accountability, and Culture

The successful implementation of net positive strategies requires strong and sustained executive leadership, clear board accountability, and a supportive organizational culture. These internal factors are foundational to embedding regeneration and inclusion across all levels of a company, ensuring that ambition is matched with execution.

Executive leadership sets the tone for how seriously an organization pursues its sustainability goals. Leaders who prioritize net positive thinking demonstrate this through clear communication, strategic alignment, and consistent decision-making. They embed environmental and social objectives into business strategy, ensure alignment with stakeholder expectations, and empower teams to act on shared goals. Leadership in this context is not just about vision—it's about operationalizing purpose and removing barriers to change.

Effective executives recognize that sustainability is not an add-on but a core business driver. They are willing to invest in innovation, reallocate resources, and rethink traditional metrics of success. This includes integrating net positive outcomes into KPIs, business unit scorecards, and financial planning processes. Leaders must also navigate trade-offs, balancing short-term pressures with long-term value creation, and be transparent about progress and challenges.

Boards of directors play a critical role in providing oversight, setting tone at the top, and holding executives accountable for sustainability performance. A net positive approach requires that boards move beyond traditional fiduciary models focused solely on financial returns, and instead embrace broader responsibilities to stakeholders and planetary systems. This shift is increasingly supported by evolving legal interpretations of fiduciary duty and investor expectations for ESG oversight.

Board-level accountability can be strengthened through dedicated sustainability committees, regular impact reporting, and integration of ESG metrics into executive compensation schemes. Diversity on boards—including representation from women, Indigenous peoples, and communities affected by corporate operations—also helps bring a wider range of perspectives and priorities into governance decisions.

Organizational culture is the connective tissue that translates leadership vision into everyday behavior. A culture aligned with net positive goals fosters collaboration, innovation, and a shared sense of purpose. It encourages employees to think systemically, challenge assumptions, and take ownership of sustainability performance in their roles.

Building such a culture requires intentional efforts, including internal communications that link company goals to societal outcomes, leadership training focused on regenerative thinking, and mechanisms that reward experimentation and continuous improvement. Employee engagement initiatives, sustainability ambassadors, and cross-functional impact teams can help bridge silos and activate change across departments.

Importantly, culture is shaped by both formal policies and informal norms. Signals from leadership—such as where resources are allocated, how decisions are made, and what behaviors are celebrated—reinforce what the organization truly values. A consistent message that sustainability is a core expectation helps institutionalize change.

Together, executive leadership, board accountability, and organizational culture form a critical internal foundation for delivering on net positive ambitions. When aligned, they ensure that sustainability is not just a public commitment, but a core element of how the organization thinks, operates, and evolves over time.

Transitioning Legacy Businesses to Net Positive Models

Legacy businesses—those with long-established operations, infrastructure, and supply chains—face distinct challenges in shifting toward net positive models. Often built on extractive or linear practices, these companies must navigate the complex process of transforming systems, retraining workforces, managing legacy assets, and updating stakeholder expectations. Despite these hurdles, legacy businesses are also well-positioned to lead, given their scale, resources, and influence across industries.

The transition begins with a comprehensive assessment of current impacts. This includes mapping environmental footprints, social risks, and dependencies across the value chain. Understanding where harm is concentrated—and where opportunities for regeneration exist—allows companies to set realistic baselines and define science-based targets for improvement. Many legacy businesses already report on emissions and resource use, but net positive models require broader, systems-level assessments that include biodiversity, water, equity, and community wellbeing.

Once baselines are established, companies can begin a phased transformation. This often includes prioritizing early wins—such as improving energy efficiency, redesigning packaging, or reducing waste—while building momentum for deeper, long-term shifts. Capital planning cycles, asset retirement timelines, and contractual obligations must be factored into transition strategies, ensuring that change is economically viable and operationally feasible.

Innovation and re-engineering are central to legacy transformation. This may involve investing in new technologies, retrofitting facilities, adopting circular models, or pivoting product lines. For example, a traditional manufacturing firm may shift from selling physical goods to offering services or performance-based contracts that reduce material intensity and support closed-loop systems.

Workforce engagement and reskilling are critical. Employees accustomed to legacy practices need training and support to adapt to new roles, technologies, and performance expectations. Just transition principles—ensuring that workers are not left behind during structural shifts—are especially relevant in high-impact sectors such as energy, transport, and heavy industry.

Stakeholder communication is also essential. Customers, investors, regulators, and communities must understand why the transition is happening, what it entails, and how progress will be measured. Transparency builds trust and allows stakeholders to play a constructive role in supporting the change. Third-party certifications, sustainability reporting, and scenario-based disclosures help demonstrate credibility.

In some cases, transitioning to net positive models requires divesting from non-aligned business units or phasing out harmful products. These decisions can be difficult but may be necessary to achieve long-term alignment with planetary boundaries and social foundations. Where divestment is not feasible in the near term, legacy businesses can offset impacts through regenerative investments, while planning for eventual transformation or exit.

Importantly, legacy companies bring advantages to the table. Their scale, infrastructure, and market access provide leverage to influence supply chains, shape industry standards, and collaborate on systemic change. Many have robust governance structures and access to capital, which can support innovation and resilience in the face of shifting expectations.

Transitioning a legacy business to a net positive model is not about achieving perfection overnight. It is about committing to a long-term pathway of improvement, transparency, and accountability. With strategic planning, inclusive leadership, and sustained effort, legacy businesses can evolve to become regenerative leaders in the next economy.

Stakeholder Engagement and Internal Transformation

Stakeholder engagement is fundamental to building the trust, legitimacy, and collective momentum needed for internal transformation toward a Net Positive Economy. Engaging stakeholders—both internal and external—not only supports transparency and accountability but also fosters collaboration and innovation across complex systems of influence.

External stakeholders include customers, investors, suppliers, governments, NGOs, Indigenous groups, and local communities. Each group brings different perspectives, expectations, and knowledge that can inform better decision-making and improve impact outcomes. A net positive approach moves beyond transactional interactions to cultivate long-term, relational engagement based on mutual respect, continuous dialogue, and shared value creation.

For example, working closely with communities affected by operations enables companies to co-develop regeneration strategies that reflect local priorities. Partnering with investors to align financing with environmental and social performance builds alignment and trust. Engaging suppliers on sustainability targets strengthens performance across the value chain and unlocks innovation. Importantly, engagement must be inclusive, ensuring that marginalized voices—such as youth, women, and Indigenous peoples—are heard and represented in shaping decisions.

Internal transformation is equally essential. Achieving net positive goals requires more than executive mandates—it depends on embedding new mindsets, behaviors, and practices across all levels of the organization. Employees must understand how their roles contribute to broader impact objectives, and they must be equipped with the skills, resources, and support to implement change.

This begins with internal communications that clearly convey the organization's vision, targets, and rationale for transformation. Purposeful messaging, storytelling, and leadership visibility help build buy-in and foster a shared sense of direction. Internal campaigns, knowledge-sharing platforms, and all-hands meetings can create feedback loops that surface ideas and identify implementation barriers early.

Training and capacity building are vital. Teams need access to tools and learning opportunities that build literacy in regenerative design, systems thinking, and social impact measurement. Sustainability training should be tailored to departments—finance, procurement, marketing, operations—so that each function understands its contribution and accountability.

Employee engagement mechanisms—such as sustainability champions, innovation labs, cross-functional task forces, or impact-focused incentives—help drive change from within. Recognizing and rewarding teams for regenerative and inclusive achievements reinforces the behaviors that support transformation. Peer-to-peer learning and internal collaboration can spark new initiatives and deepen ownership of sustainability goals.

Cultural change is often the hardest part of transformation. Legacy norms, internal silos, or resistance to change can hinder progress. Addressing these barriers requires patient leadership, consistent reinforcement, and mechanisms for feedback and adaptation. Periodic cultural assessments and employee surveys can help track progress and inform course corrections.

Finally, integration of stakeholder insights into governance, strategy, and impact reporting ensures that engagement is not symbolic but substantive. Transparency in how feedback informs decisions, and responsiveness to concerns, strengthens credibility and encourages continued participation.

When stakeholder engagement and internal transformation are aligned, organizations are better positioned to deliver on their net positive commitments. They become more adaptive, inclusive, and resilient—qualities that are essential to thriving in a rapidly changing global economy.

Chapter 9: Cultural Shift and Consumer Engagement

This chapter explores the cultural and behavioral dimensions of the Net Positive Economy. It examines how stewardship values, education, media, and storytelling can influence norms and support regenerative living. The chapter discusses behavioral economics, ethical marketing, and responsible consumption, while highlighting the role of social movements and citizen engagement in scaling sustainable practices. It concludes by framing individuals as co-creators of systemic change.

Shaping a Culture of Stewardship and Regenerative Living

A Net Positive Economy depends not only on institutional and technological change, but on a broad-based cultural shift that redefines how individuals and societies relate to nature, resources, and one another. This shift involves moving from a mindset of consumption and control toward one of stewardship, interdependence, and regeneration—where people see themselves as active participants in restoring the planet and strengthening communities.

Cultural norms shape collective behavior. They influence what is considered desirable, acceptable, or aspirational in areas ranging from lifestyle choices and career paths to consumption habits and civic engagement. In recent decades, dominant norms in many societies have promoted material consumption, speed, disposability, and individualism—values that have contributed to ecological degradation and social fragmentation.

In a Net Positive context, new cultural narratives are needed to support values of care, reciprocity, resilience, and sufficiency. This includes celebrating local knowledge, traditional practices, and Indigenous worldviews that emphasize harmony with ecosystems. It also means elevating stories of restoration, equity, and innovation that inspire collective action and reinforce the possibility of positive change.

Education systems, media, art, and popular culture are key vehicles for cultural transformation. School curricula that integrate ecological literacy, systems thinking, and civic responsibility help shape the next generation of regenerative leaders. Films, music, and visual storytelling can make abstract sustainability concepts tangible and emotionally resonant. Cultural institutions—such as museums, libraries, and community centers—serve as platforms for dialogue and learning.

Religious and spiritual traditions also play a role. Many faiths include teachings that emphasize care for creation, social justice, and humility. Engaging with these values can help mobilize moral and ethical commitments to regeneration across diverse communities.

The built environment influences culture by shaping daily experiences. Cities, neighborhoods, and public spaces designed to prioritize nature, equity, and connection can encourage regenerative behaviors and foster a sense of place. Community gardens, shared mobility, local markets, and inclusive green spaces are all examples of how infrastructure can support cultural norms rooted in stewardship.

Business and policy leaders can help accelerate cultural change by demonstrating that regenerative lifestyles are not only necessary but desirable. Marketing campaigns, brand storytelling, and product design can shift aspirations from ownership to access, from accumulation to purpose, from convenience to care. Governments can support cultural transformation through public awareness campaigns, participatory planning, and investments in cultural infrastructure.

Importantly, cultural change is not uniform or linear. It unfolds differently across geographies, generations, and social groups. A Net

Positive Economy recognizes and embraces this diversity, working with cultural contexts rather than imposing one-size-fits-all models.

By shaping a culture of stewardship and regenerative living, societies can create the social foundations needed for ecological recovery, economic inclusion, and human wellbeing. This cultural transformation is not an afterthought—it is a prerequisite for lasting systems change.

Role of Education, Media, and Storytelling

Education, media, and storytelling are essential drivers of cultural transformation toward a Net Positive Economy. They shape public understanding, influence attitudes, and provide the frameworks through which individuals and societies make sense of the world. When intentionally aligned with regenerative principles, these domains can amplify awareness, foster empathy, and catalyze large-scale behavioral and systems change.

Education equips individuals with the knowledge and skills needed to participate in and shape a regenerative future. Integrating sustainability, systems thinking, and ecological literacy into school curricula enables young people to understand interdependence between human and natural systems from an early age. Education for sustainable development (ESD) also promotes critical thinking, collaboration, and civic responsibility—key competencies for regenerative citizenship.

At the tertiary level, universities and technical institutions play a role in preparing professionals for careers in the Net Positive Economy. This includes programs in regenerative agriculture, circular economy design, sustainable finance, renewable energy, and social entrepreneurship. Interdisciplinary learning approaches help students bridge technical, social, and ethical dimensions of sustainability challenges.

Media serves as both a mirror and a catalyst for cultural change. News outlets, online platforms, documentaries, podcasts, and influencers all shape public discourse and can either reinforce or challenge dominant norms. Media coverage of climate change, social inequality, and environmental degradation has helped raise global awareness, but it often emphasizes crisis over solutions. To support net positive goals, media content must also highlight stories of hope, progress, and innovation.

Positive media narratives can showcase how businesses, communities, and individuals are regenerating ecosystems, restoring equity, or driving systemic change. This can help counter feelings of disempowerment and inspire broader participation. Responsible journalism, editorial independence, and investment in public-interest media are important to ensure credibility and diversity of perspective.

Storytelling—through film, literature, art, and personal narratives—is one of the most powerful tools for engaging emotions, shifting worldviews, and building shared meaning. Stories make abstract concepts relatable and complex systems understandable. They humanize data, illustrate trade-offs, and provide vision for what a regenerative future can look and feel like.

Storytelling is especially important in elevating voices that have historically been marginalized, including Indigenous communities, frontline environmental defenders, and youth activists. Their experiences, wisdom, and perspectives add depth to the conversation and help expand our collective imagination.

Organizations and institutions can use storytelling to communicate purpose, build trust, and strengthen engagement. This includes case studies, impact reports, employee testimonials, and community narratives. The most effective stories are authentic, inclusive, and grounded in real-world impact.

When education, media, and storytelling work together, they form a cultural infrastructure for the Net Positive Economy. They foster informed, engaged, and empowered individuals capable of driving change in their own spheres of influence—whether as voters, consumers, entrepreneurs, or community leaders.

Behavioral Economics and Nudging Sustainable Choices

While policy, technology, and infrastructure are critical for advancing a Net Positive Economy, individual behavior plays a significant role in shaping environmental and social outcomes. Behavioral economics—the study of how people make decisions—offers insights into how to encourage sustainable choices through subtle changes in context, or "nudges," that influence behavior without restricting options.

Traditional economic models assume that people act rationally and respond predictably to incentives. However, behavioral research shows that individuals are often influenced by cognitive biases, social norms, default settings, and emotional triggers. These insights can be used to design interventions that align personal decision-making with broader sustainability goals.

Nudging involves adjusting the choice architecture—the way options are presented—to make sustainable behaviors easier, more attractive, or more socially accepted. For example, setting plant-based meals as the default in cafeterias, rather than as an optional alternative, can significantly increase uptake without removing freedom of choice. Similarly, automatically enrolling employees into green pension funds—with the option to opt out—can boost investment in sustainable finance.

Visual cues, such as energy usage dashboards that compare household consumption to neighbors, can activate social comparison and encourage conservation. Labeling products with clear, standardized environmental and social impact indicators helps consumers make informed decisions quickly. Framing sustainability messages in terms of personal benefit (e.g., health, cost savings) as well as environmental impact can increase motivation.

Timing and convenience also matter. Making recycling bins more accessible than trash bins, or placing healthy and sustainable products at eye level, reduces friction and increases uptake. Digital platforms can leverage push notifications, gamification, and progress tracking to reinforce positive behaviors over time.

Behavioral approaches are especially effective when they are context-specific and culturally sensitive. What works in one community or demographic may not be effective elsewhere. Co-designing interventions with target audiences ensures that nudges are relevant, respectful, and inclusive.

However, nudging is not a substitute for regulation or structural change. It is most effective when combined with policy, infrastructure, and economic incentives that reinforce desired behaviors. For example, nudging individuals to conserve water is more effective when paired with tiered water pricing and smart metering.

Ethical considerations are important. Nudges should promote autonomy, transparency, and informed choice. They must avoid manipulation or coercion, especially when applied in areas that affect health, financial wellbeing, or access to essential services. Clear communication about the purpose and design of behavioral interventions enhances legitimacy and public trust.

In the context of a Net Positive Economy, behavioral economics offers a practical toolkit for accelerating adoption of sustainable lifestyles, consumption patterns, and civic behaviors. When thoughtfully applied, nudges can help bridge the gap between intention and action—moving individual choices toward regenerative and inclusive outcomes.

Responsible Consumption and Ethical Marketing

The transition to a Net Positive Economy depends in part on reshaping patterns of consumption—what people buy, how they use resources, and what they expect from businesses. Central to this is the promotion of responsible consumption and the adoption of ethical marketing practices that inform, empower, and align consumer choices with regenerative and inclusive outcomes.

Responsible consumption involves making purchasing and lifestyle decisions that minimize harm and, where possible, contribute to positive environmental and social impacts. This extends beyond individual product choices to broader behaviors such as reducing waste, prioritizing quality over quantity, sharing resources, and supporting companies with transparent and accountable practices.

In a net positive framework, responsible consumption is not framed solely as personal sacrifice, but as a contribution to collective wellbeing and long-term sustainability. Consumers are encouraged to view themselves as citizens with the power to shape markets and influence corporate behavior through their everyday choices.

Businesses play a key role in enabling responsible consumption. This includes offering durable, repairable, and reusable products; providing clear and accurate information on environmental and social impacts; and supporting take-back schemes or circular models. Transparency about sourcing, labor practices, and product life cycles helps consumers align their values with their purchases.

Ethical marketing ensures that communications and promotional activities are honest, inclusive, and designed to support informed decision-making. It avoids misleading claims, greenwashing, and manipulative tactics that exploit consumer concerns without delivering real impact. Ethical marketing highlights a company's sustainability efforts while acknowledging limitations and areas for improvement.

Certification labels, sustainability ratings, and product impact disclosures can support ethical marketing when backed by credible standards and third-party verification. Storytelling can also be effective—humanizing supply chains, showcasing regenerative practices, and building emotional connections to purpose. However, authenticity is critical. Consumers are increasingly adept at spotting superficial claims and expect consistency between brand messaging and business practices.

Digital platforms have amplified both the opportunities and risks of marketing. Personalized advertising, influencer partnerships, and algorithmic targeting can be used to promote sustainable products—but they must respect privacy, avoid bias, and be transparent about data use. Companies also have a responsibility to monitor how their marketing practices influence overconsumption or unsustainable norms, such as fast fashion or single-use convenience.

Equity in access is an important aspect of responsible consumption. Sustainable and ethical products must be available and affordable to a wide range of consumers. Businesses can support this through inclusive pricing strategies, community partnerships, or tiered product offerings that meet diverse needs without compromising core sustainability standards.

Governments and civil society also play a role in shaping consumption patterns—through awareness campaigns, education, and policy tools that encourage demand for responsible goods and services.

By aligning marketing and product strategies with regenerative principles, companies can support consumers in becoming active participants in the Net Positive Economy. In turn, empowered consumers can reward businesses that lead with integrity and purpose—creating a virtuous cycle of demand and innovation for sustainability.

Building Movements Around Net Positive Lifestyles

To achieve the scale and momentum required for a Net Positive Economy, individual behavior must be supported by broader social movements that normalize and celebrate net positive lifestyles. These movements bring together individuals, communities, organizations, and networks that share a commitment to regenerative living, equitable systems, and long-term wellbeing for both people and the planet.

A net positive lifestyle is characterized by choices that reduce personal ecological footprints while contributing to broader social and environmental benefits. This includes behaviors such as minimizing waste, choosing sustainable transportation, reducing consumption of high-impact goods, supporting ethical businesses, conserving energy and water, and engaging in community resilience initiatives.

However, widespread adoption of these practices depends not only on personal motivation or awareness, but on social reinforcement, shared identity, and collective action. Social movements help shift norms by creating communities of practice where sustainable choices are visible, supported, and celebrated.

Grassroots initiatives, often led by youth, Indigenous groups, and civil society organizations, have played a central role in catalyzing lifestyle-based movements. Examples include zero-waste communities, climate strikes, local food networks, ethical fashion campaigns, and repair cafes. These efforts build momentum through visibility, peer-to-peer learning, and the demonstration of tangible impact.

Digital platforms enhance the reach and coordination of net positive movements. Social media campaigns, online challenges, and community apps help individuals connect, share stories, and mobilize around shared goals. Influencers and thought leaders who authentically promote regenerative living can inspire large audiences and bring new demographics into the conversation.

Cultural institutions—such as schools, faith groups, libraries, and media outlets—can act as hubs for community learning and engagement. When these institutions adopt and promote net positive values, they help embed sustainability into daily life and strengthen intergenerational connections around stewardship and equity.

Importantly, movements must be inclusive and accessible. Regenerative lifestyles should not be positioned as elite, niche, or morally superior. Instead, they must reflect the diverse realities and constraints of different communities. Movement-building efforts should avoid judgmental framing and instead focus on empowerment, dignity, and mutual support.

Partnerships with businesses and policymakers can amplify the impact of grassroots efforts. When companies support consumer-led initiatives through sponsorship, co-creation, or product innovation, they help scale sustainable lifestyles. Similarly, public institutions can respond to citizen action by adjusting policies, investing in supportive infrastructure, or integrating movement goals into planning processes.

By building movements around net positive lifestyles, societies foster a sense of collective purpose and agency. These movements make sustainability visible and aspirational, helping individuals see themselves as part of a broader shift toward a regenerative future.

Empowering Citizens as Co-Creators of Regenerative Futures

In a Net Positive Economy, individuals are not merely consumers or beneficiaries—they are co-creators of systems that regenerate the environment and promote social wellbeing. Empowering citizens to take on this role requires more than information or incentives; it demands meaningful opportunities to participate in shaping decisions, designing solutions, and driving collective action.

Citizens are already contributing to regeneration in diverse ways: through community energy cooperatives, neighborhood greening projects, social enterprises, and participatory urban planning. These initiatives succeed when people are supported with the tools, knowledge, and governance mechanisms they need to act effectively and inclusively.

Civic participation is one pathway to co-creation. Mechanisms such as participatory budgeting, citizen assemblies, and community-led planning allow people to influence how public resources are used and which priorities are pursued. These democratic processes not only improve outcomes but also build legitimacy, trust, and a sense of ownership over regenerative transitions.

Policy design can enhance citizen empowerment by institutionalizing access to decision-making spaces, protecting the rights of marginalized groups, and ensuring transparency and responsiveness in governance. Legal frameworks that recognize community rights to land, water, and resources are particularly important for Indigenous peoples and rural populations whose traditional knowledge and stewardship practices are vital for regeneration.

Technology and data can support citizen co-creation when designed with accessibility and equity in mind. Open-source platforms, civic tech tools, and community science initiatives allow people to contribute to data collection, monitor environmental conditions, or co-design policy solutions. These tools work best when complemented by offline engagement and capacity building, especially in digitally underserved areas.

Education and skills development help citizens participate meaningfully. Regenerative futures require not just technical expertise, but competencies in systems thinking, collaboration, and leadership. Schools, community organizations, and adult education programs can all play a role in fostering active and informed citizenship.

Inclusive engagement is critical. Structural inequalities based on income, gender, race, geography, or ability can limit who is heard and who benefits. Empowerment efforts must actively remove barriers to participation and recognize the diversity of experiences, priorities, and contributions. This includes supporting language accessibility, child care, and stipends for participation in planning or governance processes.

When citizens are seen and treated as co-creators, the process of building a Net Positive Economy becomes more resilient, democratic, and effective. Public enthusiasm and creativity are harnessed, local knowledge is respected, and solutions are more likely to reflect lived realities.

Ultimately, empowering citizens is not just a means to an end—it is part of the transformation itself. A regenerative future is one in which people feel agency over their lives, stewardship over their environments, and connection to the systems that sustain them.

Conclusion

The Net Positive Economy represents a fundamental rethinking of how value is defined, created, and distributed. It challenges institutions, businesses, and individuals to go beyond minimizing harm—to contribute actively and measurably to the regeneration of natural systems and the strengthening of social foundations. In contrast to traditional models focused on efficiency or compliance, a net positive approach calls for outcomes that restore, renew, and include.

This book has outlined the principles, strategies, and tools required to make that shift. It has examined how organizations can measure net positive impact across environmental and social dimensions; how resources can be used regeneratively; how value creation must prioritize equity; and how finance, innovation, governance, and corporate leadership must evolve to support long-term resilience. It has also emphasized the cultural and behavioral changes necessary to make regeneration and inclusion part of everyday life.

At the heart of this transformation is the recognition that economies are embedded in society and nature—not separate from them. When ecosystems degrade or inequality rises, economic systems become more fragile. Conversely, when people are empowered and the environment is restored, the foundations of prosperity are strengthened. The Net Positive Economy offers a framework for reconciling growth with planetary boundaries and human rights.

Achieving this future will not be easy. It will require persistence, adaptability, and unprecedented levels of coordination across sectors and scales. Trade-offs will need to be managed, vested interests challenged, and historical inequities addressed. But the cost of inaction is higher. As climate impacts intensify, ecosystems decline, and social divides deepen, the urgency of systems change becomes clear.

Leadership will come from many directions: public institutions aligning policy with long-term goals; companies embedding purpose into strategy; financial actors directing capital toward regenerative investments; communities driving grassroots change; and individuals choosing to live in ways that support the common good. No single actor can deliver a net positive future alone—but together, collective ambition can reshape what is possible.

As this transition unfolds, transparency, accountability, and collaboration must remain central. Metrics that reflect true impact, inclusive governance structures, and open channels for dialogue and feedback will ensure that progress is real, equitable, and enduring. In doing so, we can build an economy that does more than sustain—it replenishes, uplifts, and leaves the world better for future generations.

A Net Positive Economy is not a distant ideal—it is a practical, evolving framework for redesigning systems around the outcomes we want to achieve. It is a pathway not just to survive within limits, but to thrive within them. The challenge now is to turn intention into action and ambition into measurable, lasting change.

www.ingramcontent.com/pod-product-compliance
Lightning Source LLC
Chambersburg PA
CBHW071745200326
41519CB00021BC/6874